Human Rights, Iranian Migrants, and State Media

This book offers a detailed analysis of the Islamic Republic of Iran's approach toward human rights in the media. It looks at the state-owned and state-controlled Islamic Republic of Iran Broadcasting (IRIB), employing content analysis and multimodal critical discourse analysis to explore its underlying strategies in portraying the international rights norms. The book also features analysis of surveys and interviews of recent Iranian migrants to determine the extent to which the Iranian public is aware of human rights principles and their views on whether and how the international rights norms are portrayed on IRIB.

Shabnam Moinipour has a PhD in human rights and media communications and an MA in theory and practice of human rights. She has been a visiting lecturer at the University of Westminster and a researcher at various human rights organizations including Open Doors International, Iran Human Rights Documentation Center, and the Human Rights in Iran Unit.

Routledge Studies in Media, Communication, and Politics

Human Rights, Iranian Migrants, and State Media
From Media Portrayal to Civil Reality

Shabnam Moinipour

Routledge
Taylor & Francis Group

LONDON AND NEW YORK

First published 2020 by Routledge

2 Park Square, Milton Park, Abingdon, Oxon OX14 4RN

605 Third Avenue, New York, NY 10017

Routledge is an imprint of the Taylor & Francis Group, an informa business

First issud in paperback 2021

Publisher's Note

The publisher has gone to great lengths to ensure the quality of this reprint but points out that some imperfections in the original copies may be apparent.

Library of Congress Cataloging-in-Publication Data
Names: Moinipour, Shabnam, author.
Title: Human rights, Iranian migrants, and state media: from media portrayal to civil reality / by Shabnam Moinipour.
Description: London; New York, NY: Routledge, 2019. |
Series: Routledge studies in media, communication, and politics: digitizing democracy | Includes bibliographical references and index.
Identifiers: LCCN 2019021343 |
Subjects: LCSH: Human rights in mass media. | Television broadcasting of news—Political aspects—Iran. | Såazmåan-i òSadåa va Såimåa-yi Jumhåuråi-i Islåamåi-i åIråan. | Mass media policy—Iran. | Human rights—Iran.
Classification: LCC P96.H852 I755 2019 | DDC 323.0955—dc23
LC record available at https://lccn.loc.gov/2019021343

ISBN: 978-0-367-02327-0 (hbk)
ISBN: 978-1-03-217790-8 (pbk)
DOI: 10.4324/9780429400209

Typeset in Times New Roman
by codeMantra

I dedicate this book to my loving husband, Kambiz and my dear son, Shayegan.

Contents

Figures

Tables

Abbreviations

CA	Content Analysis
CEDAW	The Convention on the Elimination of All Forms of Discrimination Against Women
CRC	The Convention on the Rights of the Child
CRPD	The Convention on the Rights of Persons with Disabilities
ICCPR	International Covenant on Civil and Political Rights
ICERD	International Covenant on Elimination of Racial Discrimination
ICESCR	International Covenant on Economic, Social and Cultural Rights
IRIB	Islamic Republic of Iran Broadcasting
MCDA	Multimodal Critical Discourse Analysis
NIRT	National Iranian Radio and Television
UDHR	Universal Declaration of Human Rights
UN	United Nations

1 Human Rights and Media: Contemporary Authoritarian Iran

The Issue at Hand

Following a long history of injustices emanating from global historical invasions and wars, which reached their climax in the 20th century with the two world wars, human rights were officially born and institutionalized at the global level with the founding of the United Nations (UN) in 1945. The UN charter was "the first international mechanism that incorporated human rights as a concept and made the promotion and protection of those rights one of the purposes of" not only individuals but also the "collective obligations of states" (1). Since then, human rights have become an ongoing dialogue between various entities and states, which are morally and legally obligated to not only protect their citizens from human rights violations but also promote human rights principles. Even though the UN does not have enforcement powers, for most states, Iran included, keeping a good image in the international community is of utmost importance. Many individuals and organizations scrutinize human rights within Iran. However, the Iranian regime is in such gross violation of citizens' rights that the promotion of human rights principles by Iran is hardly ever closely examined. The scrutiny of the promotional aspect of international human rights law is one of the gaps that this book intends to fill.

Intertwined with the above is the careful analysis of the state media in Iran. How much power the media has is unknown. Contrary to what some scholars believe, it is difficult to measure the influence and effect they have on people. However, the media, undeniably, has a force that shifts individual opinions one way or another. The Nazis were a great example of a state power using the available means of communication. They were masters of propaganda and exploited "the media of the press, cinema, and especially radio to attract support and create a consensus around their regime" (2). The definition of propaganda employed by the Iranian regime resembles that of the Nazis—articulating a few fundamental viewpoints through prescribed clichés and repeating it so much so that the forgetful masses would engrave it in their hearts.

The 1979 Islamic Revolution rendered Iran hybrid, which means that the political system landed on the overlap between democracy and authoritarianism. This hybridity has caused both democratic and authoritarian elements to exist in the country. This hybridity, in turn, has created ambiguities in the political system, which helps the regime function within a complex and diverse society.

Formal communications in Iran are entirely regime-owned and controlled. Despite this control, the Iranian regime, as is expected in an authoritarian setting, uses coercion to clamp down on journalists, bloggers, and social media users. However, every clampdown seems to have a ripple effect, which strengthens resistances in the society. Otherwise, the consensual hegemony created through the continuous blocking of communication applications such as LINE, WhatsApp, and Tango and the expansion of "smart filtering" has no other explanation. Such resistance on the part of the public adds to the complexity of Iran if we are to believe that it is the citizens of an authoritarian nation who, themselves, contribute to the survival of an "existing hegemony" based on an "established reciprocal relationship," which are ideological and material in nature (3). It is, therefore, necessary to also carefully look at the Iranian community and determine what they think of human rights as portrayed by Iran's propaganda machine.

This book examines human rights in Iran—how the Islamic Republic of Iran Broadcasting (IRIB) portrays them and how Iranians perceive them. It does so only based on the core instruments to which Iran is committed and on humanitarian norms and *jus cogens*. *Jus cogens* belong to a doctrine of international law, which "asserts the existence of fundamental legal norms from which no derogation is permitted" (4).

The Islamic Republic of Iran has committed itself to human rights through its membership to the UN and by remaining a signatory to five core international instruments: The International Covenant on Elimination of Racial Discrimination, the International Covenant on Civil and Political Rights, the International Covenant on Economic, Social and Cultural Rights, the Convention on the Rights of the Child, and the Convention on the Rights of Persons with Disabilities (5). The study of the IRIB is of utmost importance since, as a form of mass communication and as the regime-owned and controlled apparatus, it is meant to be used for the promotion and propagation of human rights principles as per the UN Charter.

IRIB: Television News

The state-run television as part of IRIB was chosen as the focus of this research not only because IRIB is the most highly funded media outlet in the country (6), but also because, according to the Iran Media Program of the University of Pennsylvania, which carried out a field-based study in four major metropolitan cities in Iran (Tehran, Mashhad, Tabriz, and Shiraz), television, radio, and the press, as traditional forms of news media, were preferred over new forms of news media such as the Internet, text message, or social media by the participants. A full 96% of the people queried in the study[1] cited television news as their most important news source (7). People do use other forms of mass communications in Iran, such as telephone, cellular mobiles, the Internet, radio, and newspapers. Internet use is particularly on the rise (8). However, even though people in Iran use other forms of communication like the Internet and satellite dishes to connect with the outside world and catch up with political and world affairs, they frequently face severe crackdowns by the regime. Thus, state-controlled television remains the primary source of information for many Iranians (9). Empirical data have shown that television has impacted public opinion on human rights (10). For this research, which seeks to explore public perceptions of Iranians on human rights, television is a more appropriate medium for analysis.

The views of IRIB are concurrent with those of the Iranian regime. IRIB, as a whole, is used by the Iranian regime as a "broadcasting pulpit" (11). The pulpit or *minbar* is a place in the mosque where religious figures address or preach to the masses. Preaching has been a systematized and keen form of communication and interaction with the public for many centuries (12). It has been used to "inform," "guide," and "agitate" (11). Television, therefore, is a propaganda machine, a unique medium that delivers state messages nationwide. It is unique because, according to research, "television is essentially and fundamentally different from other forms of mass media" (13). Literacy is not a requirement for television viewing, unlike newspapers, magazines, and books. Unlike movies, television is free. Unlike radio, television combines pictures and sound. Mobility is not required. People of all ages can interact with television, and it is accessible and available to everyone (13). The interaction is one-way, however, which makes the study of television relatively easier. Some scholars argue that texts should not be studied in isolation but that images should also be analyzed (14). Thus, this research focuses on content analysis (CA) and multimodal critical discourse analysis

(MCDA) to examine the Islamic Republic of Iran's practices of news production using the international human rights law as the legal framework.

If the Iranian regime is found to abuse the principles of international human rights law for propaganda purposes, then this research intends to establish how it does it and how the results correlate with the Iranian migrants' opinions on the subject.

Human Rights, Television, and the Iranian Public

Due to the nature of authoritarianism and the political climate in Iran, researching the Iranian public comes with certain challenges and inhibitions. The ethical issues associated with researching human subjects are so overbearing that they may negatively influence the study or halt it altogether. To safeguard the well-being of the participants but allow them freedom to express their opinions, recent Iranian migrants were chosen as the participants for this research. Another reason for this selection was the temporal dimension of their status. They were recent enough to remember what they watched on television yet not old enough to be part of the established Iranian diaspora.

The surveys and interviews discussed here were conducted between May 14 and August 11, 2015. Recent Iranian migrants residing in the United Kingdom and Canada were the focus group of this study. Based on the UK government's statistical report on immigration, Iran was ranked second among nationalities applying for asylum in 2015 (15). In the same year, Iran was the fourth largest source of immigrants to Canada (16), according to *The Canadian Magazine of Immigration*. Recent Iranian immigrants in both the UK and Canada were selected randomly through nonprobability sampling, which did not guarantee that all recent immigrants had an equal chance of participating (17). For this research, *recent immigrant* refers to any Iranian individual who had immigrated to a destination country, in this case, Britain and Canada, within five years from the time of the interview and survey conductions. Both the Canadian and the UK governments consider an individual a newcomer until they become eligible to apply for citizenship after five years (18, 19).

A mixed method, which includes both qualitative and quantitative methods, was used to collect data from 101 individual migrants. Individuals were chosen based on particular characteristics to enable them to respond to the research questions appropriately and in the best way possible. The participants comprised of any migrant—political dissidents, economic migrants, asylum seekers, and refugees. The participants also included short- and long-term visitors from Iran. Except for being recent immigrants and having some knowledge of the news content on national television in Iran, there were no other criteria for individuals to be eligible to participate. Individuals from any religion, gender, ethnicity, or age over 18 could participate.

The Structure and Focus of the Book

Mixed methods were used in the research laid out in this book, including CA and MCDA, to explore the underlying features of international human rights norms as portrayed on Iranian television. These two methods were used not only to determine when and under what circumstances international human rights principles are presented in the news but also to look at the images, sounds, and gestures made by the presenters to determine holistically how "social power abuse, dominance, and inequality are enacted, reproduced, and resisted by text and talk in the social and political context" (20).

Surveys and interviews were utilized to determine if the participants understand whether international human rights norms are portrayed on IRIB, whether they are aware of human rights principles, and whether they accept or reject what is portrayed on IRIB. Surveys were used as a quantitative method for data collection to measure "facts," "attitudes," and "behaviors" of the recent Iranian migrants in relation to the findings derived from CA and MCDA of the television news programs. The interviews assisted with strengthening the "understanding of agents' perspectives, social process and context" drawn from surveys (21).

This book is unique in that no prior publications have empirically sought to analyze the use of human rights principles in media in Iran and follow up with the Islamic Republic of Iran's claims on the promotion of human rights principles.

In sum, this book focuses on the following:

- The kinds of international human rights principles, customary norms, and *jus cogens* covered on IRIB news programs.
- The degree to which human rights principles, customary norms, and *jus cogens* are included in the news.
- The way human rights principles, customary norms, and *jus cogens* are presented in the news.
- The perception of recent Iranian migrants on how human rights principles get covered in the news.

- Recent Iranian migrants' understanding of human rights principles.
- Identification of any correlations between the expressions of human rights principles, customary norms, and *jus cogens* by IRIB and migrants' perception of the same principles.

This book is divided into eight chapters. This first chapter briefly examined the issue at the heart of the book, the importance of the work, the design of the research, and the outline of the book. Chapter 2 provides a theoretical and conceptual framework for the understanding of Iran and the Iranian regime after the 1979 Islamic Revolution—what it inherited from the Pahlavi dynasty and the kind of society it has attempted to mold Iran into.

Chapter 3 briefly explores the history of IRIB followed by a more in-depth discussion of the aims and policies of IRIB, its administration in relation to the state, the setup of the organization, and the news policies. The study of IRIB is of significance since the "promotion, protection, and exercise of human rights cannot effectively take place unless the right of the individual and the public to know or to be fully informed is also protected." That is why any form of mass communication is an integral part of that right (1). The chapter then looks at the specific policies of IRIB into which international human rights principles, based on the core instruments mentioned previously, have been incorporated.

Chapter 4 analyzes the actual television news programs of IRIB, employing CA based on eight general international human rights principles—right to life, right to freedom from genocide, right to freedom from discrimination, right to political participation, right to freedom of expression and association, right to freedom of assembly, protection of civilians, right of protection of journalists in conflict—selected following the application of an exploratory method. These principles were not limited to human rights. They also included specific international humanitarian laws that were either a part of customary norms or *jus cogens*. The difference lies in the fact that once established customary laws bind all states. However, human rights principles need to be ratified by states for them to become binding. There may, of course, be exceptions to this norm that this book does not discuss (22). Chapters 5 and 6 build on the results of the CA in Chapter 4 and focus on MCDA of two foreign and two domestic news packages, respectively, as reported on Iranian television.

Based on the results of Chapters 5 and 6, Chapter 7 is dedicated to the second aim of this book and analyzes the results obtained from the responses of the recent Iranian migrants through survey and conducting interviews. The chapter delves deep into the opinion of the recent migrants on and their knowledge of human rights. It is also determined in this chapter whether the migrants recognize, accept, or reject the human rights norms and principles as portrayed in the news based on the results obtained from the news analysis in Chapters 5 and 6.

The final chapter, Chapter 8, triangulates the multidisciplinary theories and concepts discussed in the book with the results obtained from the television and migrant analyses, drawing conclusions and offering multiple communication and cultural policies that could be implemented and administered by the UN and various other entities.

The importance of empirical research on the promotion of human rights in a state, whose record remains tarnished, cannot be overstated. The in-depth look at the IRIB, namely its television news programs, through the utilization of CA and MCDA fills a wide gap in the literature. The literature is also in a deficit of the human-centered designed research on the topic presented in this book in particular on Iran whose authoritarian side overweighs its occasional democratic outbursts. The surveys and interviews administered on the recent Iranian migrants in the research laid out in this book are also unique and quite significant.

Note

1 **Tehran**: total population (7,088,287), sample size (500); **Mashhad**: total population (2,427,316), sample size (200); **Tabriz**: total population (1,398,060), sample size (150); **Shiraz**: total population (1,227,331), sample size (150).

References

1. Langley W. *Encyclopedia of human rights issues since 1945*. Westport, CT: Greenwood Press; 1999:xi.
2. Nicholls D. *Adolf Hitler: A biographical companion*. Santa Barbara, CA & Oxford: ABC-CLIO; 2000:203.
3. Pratt N. Bringing politics back in: Examining the link between globalization and democratization. *Review of International Political Economy*. 2004;11(2):318.
4. Charlesworth H, Chinkin C. The gender of jus cogens. *Human Rights Quarterly*. 1993;15(1):63.
5. Moinipour S. UN treaty-based bodies and the Islamic Republic of Iran: Human rights dialogue (1990–2016). *Cogent Social Sciences*. 2018;4(1):5–6.
6. BBC Persian. *Who are appointed in Iran by the order of the Supreme Leader?* April 18, 2016. Available from: http://www.bbc.com/persian/iran/2016/04/160409_126_145_ir_leader_power_chart:12.

7. Enayat M, Smith B, Wojcieszak M. *Finding a way—How Iranians reach for news and information*. University of Pennsylvania; 2011–2012. Available from: http://www.global.asc.upenn.edu/fileLibrary/PDFs/Findinga-Way.pdf.

8. Sreberny A, Khiabany G. *Blogistan: The Internet and politics in Iran*. London: I. B. Tauris; 2010:2.

9. Freedom House. *Countries at the crossroads 2012: Iran*. Freedom House; 2012. Available from: https://freedomhouse.org/sites/default/files/Iran - FINAL.pdf:4.

10. Iyengar S. *Is anyone responsible?: How television frames political issues*. Chicago, IL & London: University of Chicago Press; 1991:4.

11. Sreberny-Mohammadi A, Mohammadi A. *Small media, big revolution: Communication, culture, and the Iranian Revolution*. Minneapolis & London: University of Minnesota Press; 1994:173 & 185.

12. Fathi A. The role of the Islamic pulpit. *Journal of Communication* 1979;29(3):16.

13. Baran SJ, Davis DK. *Mass communication theory: Foundations, ferment, and future*. 6th ed. International ed. Stamford, CT: Wadsworth Cengage Learning; 2012:342.

14. Fairclough N. A dialectical-relational approach to critical discourse analysis in social research. In: Wodak R, Meyer M, editors. *Methods of critical discourse studies*. 3rd ed. Chennai: SAGE; 2016:89.

15. ONS. *Migration statistics quarterly report: February 2016*. Office for National Statistics; 2016. Available from: http://www.ons.gov.uk/people populationandcommunity/populationandmigration/internationalmi gration/bulletins/migrationstatisticsquarterlyreport/february2016.

16. The Canadian Magazine of Immigration. *Canada: Immigration by source country (2015)*. 2016. Available from: http://canadaimmigrants.com/ canada-immigration-by-source-country-2015/.

17. Fink A. *The survey handbook*. 2nd ed. Thousand Oaks, CA; London: Sage Publications; 2003:39.

18. Government of Canada. *Understand permanent resident status*. 2014. Available from: http://www.cic.gc.ca/english/newcomers/about-pr.asp.

19. UK Government. *Become a British citizen*. 2016. Available from: https:// www.gov.uk/becoming-a-british-citizen/check-if-you-can-apply.

20. van Dijk T. Critical discourse analysis. In: Schiffrin D, Tannen D, Hamilton HE, editors. *The handbook of discourse analysis*. Malden, MA: Blackwell Publishers Ltd.; 2001:352.

21. May T. *Social research: Issues, methods and process*. 3rd ed. Buckingham: Open University Press; 2001:112.

22. Ghanea-Hercock N. *Human rights, the UN and the Bahá'is in Iran*. Oxford: George Ronald; 2002:16.

2 Human Rights, Regime Change, and Political Succession in the Post-1979 Islamic Revolution

From the Pahlavi Era to Khomeinism

Before the 1979 Islamic Revolution took place in Iran, Mohammad Reza Shah Pahlavi (1919–1981) reined over the Pahlavi dynasty, which was founded by his father, Reza Shah Pahlavi, in 1925. Mohammad Reza Shah appeared to have all that was required for sovereignty in perpetuity. He had the backing of the West, especially the United States, the financial backbone, an efficient army, and an intelligence service, i.e. SAVAK. Neither was the Shah's government the result of a war-ravaged country. The revolution, nonetheless, proved that even the pungently protected dynasty was not invincible (1). Numerous factors contributed to the Pahlavi dynasty's demise in 1979, namely the trebling of the urban population between 1956 and 1979, which is generally correlated with "increasing religious orthodoxy." The massive internal migration and growth in literacy metastasized into widespread religious activities and publications with a more significant portion of the population gaining access to Shi'ite traditionalism (2).

The accommodating and incorporative activities mentioned earlier paved the way for the society to become receptive to advocates of Shi'ite traditionalism and receive the charismatic Khomeini as its Ayatollah and the Supreme Leader of the Islamic Republic of Iran post the 1979 Islamic Revolution. How Khomeini managed to convince the majority by enforcing concepts such as *ummat* and Westoxication in a post-revolutionary contemporary form of hybrid authoritarianism and maintain gaining legitimacy from the public by staging traditionalism are points of interest of this chapter, as they lead the argument into the discussion of human rights and the nature of its existence in Iran.

Ummat *versus* Mellat

Prior to the Islamic Revolution, Iran was heavily influenced by the West. The psychological dependency created by this association was sometimes even more than the actual political or cultural influence it had over the country (3). The Pahlavi monarchs aimed to create a nation-state and a national identity, which, as the 1979 revolution proved, never gained full legitimacy from the people. This failure was partially due to secularization and modernization efforts of the Shah.

These efforts infused a national identity with a very distinct secular ideology that attempted to diminish the importance of Islam in Iran. These policies led to the gradual lessening of clerical power, which for a long time had been considerable (4). The Shah believed that the concept of nationhood was necessary for a formal state to have continuity. Mohammad Reza Shah tried to accomplish his goals by using modern media. He thought that media could play an essential part in the development of a sense of national identity (3).

When he gained power in 1979, Khomeini also aimed to create a collective national identity but one of a very different nature than that of the Shah. The problem with the Shah's efforts lay in the definition of collectivity or *mellat* (nation) as opposed to Khomeini's interpretation of collectivity or *ummat* (community) (3). *Ummat* has been referred to as the "community of the faithful" (5), which highlights its reference to a religious collectivity that Khomeini had envisioned. As an Islamic concept, *ummat* refers to a group of people who have chosen to traverse one common path together. Interestingly, this common path does not lead to an individual struggle for higher spiritual attainment or closeness to God but rather to "one common leadership" or *Imamat*. Prior to the revolution, influential Iranian intellectual and sociologist, Ali Shari'ati, revitalized the concept of *ummat*, arguing that it is the "community" that Islam regards as the holiest, most superior, and most fundamental connection between people, not the commonality in blood, ethnicity, race, nation, social status, or lifestyle (6). Shari'ati saw *ummat* as being commonly rooted with *Imamat* or leadership (6). Once in power, Khomeini immediately claimed the title of "Imam"[1] or "leader" for himself (7), utilizing the concept to his benefit.

Although Pahlavi's approach toward national identity was flawed in its definition and application, Khomeini was fully aware of its inherent usefulness for the creation of his collective solidarity. Taking into account the fact that 98% of the Iranians were Shi'a Muslims and have been for centuries, unifying the people through the concept of *ummat*, which went beyond the national boundaries and into the Islamic world, seemed an easier task (3).

The Hybridity of the Post-1979 Regime

During the regime change of 1979, both the necessary transition and transformation for the establishment of a democracy, as was initially promised by Khomeini, failed. In various interviews immediately before and after the revolution, Khomeini gave responses such as these: "Islamic state means a state based on justice and democracy and structured upon Islamic rules and laws" (8), "With people's revolutionary rage, the king will be ousted and a democratic state, Islamic Republic, will be established" (9), and "[c]heering, for me, means to love freedom and democracy" (10). As is evident, Khomeini's promises were in words alone and once the Islamic Republic was established he uttered statements such as

> Don't listen to those who speak of democracy. They all are against Islam. They want to take the nation away from its mission. We will break all the poison pens of those who speak of nationalism, democracy, and such things (11).

Even if Khomeini had pure intentions, democracy would not have been the outcome of the revolution. The outcome was not even the intended theocracy in its pure form. After the revolution, the failure to transition and to transform into democracy caused the new Iranian regime to land on a "grey area between authoritarianism and democracy" (12). Hence, the autocratic monarchy was replaced by a hybrid regime or a contemporary authoritarian regime. It is called contemporary authoritarian because there are both democratic and authoritarian elements present in Iran, but the authoritarian elements do not allow the democratic elements to flourish (13).

The first requirement for a full transition to democracy would be the enactment of policies that allow the lower classes to be politically involved in their affairs and of the country. This requirement is accomplished by redistributing the economic factors of production for the economically unprivileged people to overcome those factors contributing to their marginalization (12). In line with this transitional concept, Mohammad Reza Shah succeeded in modernizing the socioeconomic aspect of Iran; yet he failed to modernize the political aspect of it, thus rendering the political system an autocratic monarchy (14). Based on the earlier definition, an ideal situation for a successful transition is a political change from autocracy to democracy. Pahlavi had already provided the ideal situation for this change by creating an autocratic political system; yet after the 1979 Islamic Revolution such transition was not completed, and the autocratic monarchy was replaced by a hybrid regime, which is widely considered as authoritarian.

Even with the Shah's modernization efforts, the socioeconomics was also not transformed fully. The second requirement for a successful transition to democracy is a complete socioeconomic transformation, which should ideally change from "rent economy (with marginality)" to a "market economy (without marginality)[2]" (12). During Pahlavi's White Revolution (1963–1977)[3] (15), the cost of living index grew, and some land was redistributed. However, the economy developed unevenly, benefitting the rich more than the middle and lower classes, especially in larger cities like Tehran. Besides, the oil boom in the final years of the Pahlavi era merely modernized poverty since the poor were forced to migrate from villages to large cities but benefited minimally from the rapid economic growth in the country (14). However, through overseeing the movement of commodities and goods brought into the country, through assisting with the managing of businesses, and through lowering the cost of credit, the state was able to support the private sector of the market or *bazaar* to maintain a free-market system (16).

Thus, although Mohammad Reza Shah attempted to create a market economy, at the time of the revolution the country as a whole was far from fully realizing a democratic capitalist economy. Hussein Mahdavy calls this unrealized democratic capitalism, *rentierism*. Rentier states are defined as "those countries that receive on a regular basis substantial amounts of external rent. External rents are in turn defined as rentals paid by foreign individuals, concerns or governments to individuals, concerns or governments of a given country" (17). A rentier state is incapable of promoting democracy since a rentier state can distribute the revenue it obtains from external entities without the need for domestic income or taxation (18). Without taxation, democracy is not taken seriously, and there is no public dissent (18). The reason is that with taxation, representation is expected. "[T]axation without representation" may not necessarily anger the public, but a lack of service provisions by the government might. An increase in prices of such services leads to a public outcry for accountability of authoritarian regimes (19).

It is only through the destruction of the rentier economy that full democracy can be reached. Otherwise, the regime would naturally become hybrid during any transition (12). After the revolution, the systems that upheld the rentier economy were not broken down, and the economy became increasingly complex, which was publicized by the new regime as booming, fair, and independent (16). In the aftermath of the revolution, the *bazaar* was weakened to the core and ceased to be an independent entity. Instead, it became dependent on various networks outside the country that were either controlled or directed by the state. The economy grew more of a rentier economy governed by excessive state regulation of the market and a manipulated and co-erced rent distribution, designed to benefit those at the top of the hier-archy (20). Thus, the Islamic Republic of Iran became an even stronger rentier state autonomous from the society. A rentier state only needs to allocate the smallest portion of its wealth to the public for it to become indulgent with the rest. In other words, people's rights are ransomed for a small portion of the rent money that flows in from abroad (21).

The Supreme Leader sits at the top of this hierarchy. In 1979, the new regime drafted a new constitution, which was later on amended to give him "unlimited power" (22). This ultimate power has been one of the enduring aspects of the regime. The Iranian regime and the Islamic ideology it has put in place constitute an amalgam of many laws and regulations. These laws and regulations are contra-dictory with each other and are aimed to create a pure Islamic state with citizens fully obedient to Islam, to perpetuate clerical rule, (23) and to create an "ideal identity," an "ideal society," and an "ideal state." The ideologies that would conform to such idealisms based on the Sharia law were constructed in the abovementioned hybrid climate, consequently turning the regime into an ambiguous and di-chotomous entity.

Expressions of Hybridity: Ambiguity and Dichotomy

The expressions of hybridity in the fabric of the Islamic Republic of Iran are many. The discussion, however, is limited to the Iranian Con-stitution since it bears the fundamental principles of the regime's gov-ernance. In its Constitution, the Iranian regime has bestowed to all Iranians a variety of fundamental universal rights, such as freedom of speech and assembly, freedom of religion, right to education, social security, and a fair trial, to name a few. However, by placing these rights into the Constitution, a dichotomy has been created between the notions of popular sovereignty and the sovereignty of God. On the one hand, Articles 1 and 2 of the Constitution confer "longstanding belief" by the Iranian people in the "sovereignty of truth and Qur'anic justice" and sovereignty of God while on the other, Article 6 demands that the "affairs of the country must be administered on the basis of public opinion expressed by the means of elections ... or by means of referenda in matters specific in other articles of this Constitution" (24). This contradiction is the reason why the Iranian Constitution has also been called a "hybrid of authoritarian, theocratic and democratic el-ements" (25).

Another example of the expression of hybridity in the form of ambiguity and dichotomy is with regard to the Islamic belief that attributes the "ultimate sovereignty" to God (26). In Article 56 (Chapter V) of the Constitution, the sovereignty of God is explicitly recognized. It specifies that

> [a]bsolute sovereignty over the world and man belongs to God, and it is He Who has made man master of his own social destiny. No one can deprive man of this divine right, nor subordinate it to the vested interests of a particular individual or group (24).

The regime exercises the opposite of this very same article of the Constitution and proclaims that the Shi'a clergy, as God's deputies, exercises His sovereignty on earth (26). It is on this basis that Khomeini established his doctrine of *velayat-e faqih*, translated as "rule of the supreme jurist" (27). Through the creation of ideological ambiguities and dichotomies, the Iranian regime has "attempted to legitimate the on-going suppression of fundamental rights in the Islamic Republic" (28).

Some scholars believe that the dichotomy is in fact between the Iranian regime's "Islamic ideology" and "true Islamic policies and actions." In their view, the regime's Islamic ideology attempts to rally people under the banner of Islam. The clergy has made an effort to attain cultural hegemony, a process that enforces a certain direction on social life by the ruling group on the ruled (29), but to no avail. They have only succeeded in achieving a cultural hegemony among "the least educated, most economically disadvantaged, and most culturally impoverished citizens" (23). For everyone else who cannot leave Iran, "compliance with Islamic rule and the clerical cultural hegemony" has been "involuntary," "transitory," and "volatile" (23).

In response to Iran's defeat in an attempt to obtain a seat on the UN Human Rights Council in 2006, Hillel Neuer, Executive Director of UN Watch,[4] stated that "Iran's domestic and foreign policy is hostile to the very principles of human dignity and the principles of the universal declaration of human rights" (30). In general, by making the laws ambiguous and using phrases such as "except in cases sanctioned by law," "exception will be specified by law," "except as provided by law," or "except in cases provided by law," the Iranian regime has created a dichotomous situation. Consequently, its hands have been left wide open to violate its domestic laws whenever it suits it but can simultaneously show the international community that its domestic laws conform with the international human rights law.

Re-traditionalism: An Invented Tradition

The Shah's modernization efforts created confusion, which led to new ideological activities. The rapid urbanization and spread of literacy contributed to the revitalization of Shi'ism. During this time, Islamic literature, political activities, and networks grew considerably. New ideological activities are due to loss of orientation caused by responses triggered by psychological, cultural, and social stress (31). Khomeini's so-called traditional ideologies emerged from the disorientation that resulted from the Shah's move toward secularization and modernization. The restoration of past Islamic traditions was impossible because of all that had changed over centuries, but Khomeini's ideologies had to resemble at least older traditions to be accepted by the people. For their part, the clergy manufactured a new, politicized tradition that was not merely a return to traditionalism, but, rather an "ideological re-traditionalism," a term coined by anthropologist Clifford Geertz.

Social critic Alan Hunt interprets Geertz's ideological re-traditionalism as having two distinct elements. One element attempts to provide a new rationale and basis for tactics to reintroduce "traditional forms of social relations" and "respond to new and disturbing social changes." In the case of Iran, social changes, which occurred before the revolution, had undermined the authority of religious figures and marginalized their position. The second element suggests that re-traditionalization creates certain social values that are innovative in their structure (32). By establishing a unified religious nation, "tradition" became political and Khomeini's Shi'ite theology—the *velayat* or the "guardianship of the community"—was further legitimized. In addition, the occultation of the Twelfth Imam gave theologians an excuse to interfere in every aspect of public life, from social to economic to political issues, further legitimizing their status (23).

When a society goes through a rapid transformation, such as Iran faced during the Pahlavi era, older traditions that predate the transition are most often either weakened or destroyed. In the aftermath of such rapid change and with the coming of a new social order, the Islamic Republic created what scholars call an invented tradition (33). Historian Eric Hobsbawm defined an invented tradition as a "set of practices, normally governed by overtly or tacitly accepted rules and of a ritual or symbolic nature, which seek to inculcate certain values and norms of behaviour by repetition, which automatically implies continuity with the past" (33).

Further, according to Hobsbawm, a single initiator usually constructs an invented tradition. Khomeini, as the founder of the Islamic

Republic of Iran, introduced an ideology that appeared to be based on a tradition connected to an immemorial past, inherited from the Prophet Muhammad and passed on to the Imams and ultimately to the learned theologians, known as the *"Faqihs"* (23). However, since his ideology had to be "re"-traditionalized, it was not linked to any single tradition. It was, rather, designed to mimic older traditions (33).

Some scholars suggest that Shi'ite re-traditionalism or the creation of invented tradition was not a random movement that just happened to erupt in 1979. The traditionalists had a steady presence in Iran throughout its history, even as they became less dominant during times of tension and strain (34). The re-emergence of traditionalism in 1979 resulted from dissatisfaction with how the country was changing and reshaping. The Shi'ite traditionalists, therefore, offered an appealing alternative ideology that aligned with people's understandings of ancient tradition.

Westoxication

Shi'ite Islam is based on the belief that it is the master religion. Everyone in society must adhere to it for a pure culture based on a shared religious identity to emerge. The closer one gets to the Prophet Muhammad, the purer the shared identity is. Hence, most of the clergy who are *Sayyids*—descendants of the family of Mohammad—are considered purer, and they demonstrate this by wearing differently colored turbans[5] (35). In order to safeguard the pure collective religio-cultural identity that is forcefully created by the regime, the *'ulama* or the clergy, with Khomeini as their *Marja'-e Taqlid* (source of imitation), started a "traditional movement" to defend Islam against the influences of the West (34), which they firmly believed was a form of *gharbzadegi* or "Westoxication" of the nation (22). University of Tehran professor, Ahmad Fardid, coined the term *Westoxication* in the 1940s (36) to call attention to the rapid changes happening in the Iranian society. The concept is now more prominently associated with Jalal Al-e Ahmad, an eminent Iranian writer, who in 1964 popularized the term in *Occidentosis: A Plague from the West* (37). The clergy, wrote Al-e- Ahmad, thought of the West as a disease, resembling "an infestation of weevils, ... [an] accident from without, spreading in an environment rendered susceptible to it" (37).

Opponents of Westoxication were enraged by the customs associated with Western influence. They expressed disdain for modernity and democracy, which were viewed as antithetical to Islamic values (38). Through Khomeini's politicization of religion after the 1979 Revolution, rejection of Westoxication became one of the ways in which the Iranian regime gained legitimization. They were able to point to Westernization under the Shah as stripping Iranian culture of its unique identity and could propose a return to tradition that was in actuality a new invention.

Within an atmosphere that rejected secularization and outside influences and saw both as dangerous to Iranian culture, the Islamic Republic's ideology contributed to the serious setback of human rights discourse that was beginning to take shape internationally.

Radical Democracy and Antagonism

As a contemporary authoritarian state, Iran possesses both democratic and authoritarian elements. One such element is the existence of agonism and antagonism, even though the latter has almost entirely made the former non-existent. The authoritarian aspect of Iran has exacerbated antagonism not only among individual Iranians but also in public discourse and foreign relations. Agonism and antagonism are terms employed in the *radical democracy model* to describe democratic politics. The model, therefore, deserves considerable attention.

Radical democracy model is based on the concept of *the political.* Some define *the political* as a space of freedom and political discourse (39), and others define it as a space of power by "friend-enemy groupings" (40). It is the latter definition of *the political* that the radical democracy model is based on. In the radical democracy model, this political construction of friend-enemy grouping is called *antagonism*, and *the political* is defined as "the antagonistic dimension which is inherent to all human societies" (41). By contrast, politics seeks to create order, which organizes "human coexistence under conditions that are marked by *the political* and thus always conflictual" (42).

The radical democracy model rejects any model, such as the liberal theory model, that is based on the belief that differences in values and perspectives can be consolidated or reconciled. Such models require an attempt to reach a consensus in the society without excluding anyone and by eliminating potential antagonism. The radical democracy model postulates that achieving unanimity is a grievous challenge since in this scenario an "us" needs to be created that does not include an equivalent "them" (41). Societies are pluralistic, which means that there are various values and belief systems. However, the plurality that exists within a society cannot and should not be denied, according to the radical democracy model. Acceptance of plurality does not mean that differences cannot harmoniously co-exist. They can but only if the antagonistic dimension of *the political* is rejected. There is always going to be an "us" and a "them" in politics. A so-called pluralistic democratic society must recognize such differences. Therefore, conflict can exist or even should exist but in an agonistic or adversarial way (in its positive form). Therefore, in a pluralist democracy, a distinction needs to be made between "enemy" and "adversary" to overcome this challenge.

According to the radical democracy model, the more democratic a society, the more agonistic its conflicts. At the opposite end of this spectrum are the less democratic societies where the nature of the conflicts is more antagonistic. Since Iran falls on the opposite end of a democratic spectrum, antagonism may best describe its political practices.

Under non-democratic conditions such as authoritarianism, the "us" and "them" are constantly changed to "friend" and "enemy," making political practice antagonistic. This change occurs as soon as those who are categorized as being different begin to be looked upon as jeopardizing *"our* identity" and endangering *"our* existence" (41). The friend-enemy grouping is the extreme form of antagonism and the closer a state gets to the political side of the spectrum, the more antagonistic it gets. It is left to the state to decide who is the "friend" and who is the "enemy" (43). It is also the state that decides how to deal with the enemy. This power is usually exercised by providing protection for the enemy in exchange for obedience to the state (44).

Khomeini's doctrine of *velayat-e faqih* created such a power. Those who obey the Supreme Leader and conform to the Islamic religio-cultural identity as defined by the Shi'a clergy are considered as "us" and are protected from the "enemy," and those who are different and wish to remain different are labeled as "them" and are considered to be the enemy. Since religion and culture have become intertwined with politics in Iran, having a religio-cultural identity mirrors an individual's political identity. This close connection between religio-cultural values and political identities makes it extremely difficult to eradicate antagonism (41).

Hegemonic Practices

The Iranian regime has established order by defining the system through certain practices called *hegemonic practices* (41). Hegemony has been defined as the triumph of the powerful in turning their view of the world into what the passive public has consequently come to believe as the norm (45). By this definition, hegemony is non-coercive.

Others see hegemonic power as existing in reciprocity and involving more than one actor. In this definition, hegemony is not top-down domination of a powerful group or class at a cost to the rest. Hegemony's sustenance comes from the agreement on the naturalness of such power relations.

Nevertheless, such hegemony can be backed by coercion on the part of the state apparatus (46). Some states maintain control through the use of both coercion and ideology (45). Hegemony in an authoritarian setting is multidimensional and therefore must not be narrowed down to economic and institutional aspects only (47). Indeed, it is hegemony related to culture that thwarts any meaningful connection between the cause and effect of economics and political demands (47).

As part of the ideological hegemony of the Islamic Republic of Iran, the regime has created a fluid "hegemonic, official Islamic culture." The Islamic Republic has predominantly accomplished this through the use of media, the broadcasting system, and an attempt to create an "Islamic" television (48). However, after the revolution, the translation of Khomeini's ideological doctrines based on the tenets of a "pure Islam" into realistic policies has proved challenging, especially concerning media, since media did not exist at the time the Quran was revealed. In addition, the Islamicization of Iranian culture through tight control of both public and private spheres has been met with resistance. Once a nation goes through a revolution, if the governing body has an ideologically oriented rule, it will be fundamentally restricted by the structures still in place from before (49). Hence, the difficulty in Islamicizing Iranian culture could be due to how rapidly society transformed during the Shah's reign. His cultural modernization and developmental efforts had influenced the educated and the urban elites. Therefore, the will of the Islamic Republic of Iran to ideologically control the people through hegemony does not necessarily mean that they can achieve it.

In addition to their attempts at internal hegemony, the Iranian regime also attempts to apply hegemonic practices at the international level. At the macro and international level, the question of the universality of international human rights norms becomes a concern, for example. Does it exist and, more importantly, should it exist? Should cultural relativism be taken into consideration? During the United Nations Human Rights Council's Universal Periodic Review held on October 31, 2014, Mohammad-Javad Larijani, secretary general of Iran's High Council for Human Rights, stated that "we [Iran], in our approach towards human rights, will act based on gratifying Islamic principles, the Constitution and international obligations" (50).

Ideological Hegemony: Culture of Broadcasting

Even with the international human rights commitments, the current Iranian regime has maintained an oppressive ideology and continues to suppress those who do not submit to the dominant ideology. To the Iranian regime, the Islamic ideology is enshrined with the highest cultural and moral standards that benefit those who accept to them.

An ethical state is a state that raises the public to a level of cultural and moral standards that allow individuals to grow and be productive members of society. Reaching these standards should be the primary goal of the ruling class. However, once, instead of serving the interests of ordinary people, the state's goals and actions become private and gear toward serving the interests of its own, then interference occurs in an essential state function. Consequently, the wheels of *the political* and the "cultural hegemony of the ruling classes" begin to turn (45). With the politicization of religion in Iran, political and cultural hegemony became more dominant. Ostensibly to combat Westoxication, the Iranian regime uses media as a cultural tool to deliver its Islamic ideology, creating what has been called an "ideological hegemony" (48).

The process of Islamicization through rearrangement and reorganization of the broadcast media created many resistances. These resistances resulted from going against the cultural climate that was created before the revolution, ranging from "particular organizational culture," "set of trained personnel," and "already formed cultural habits." The hybrid nature of the political system, which yields ambiguous and dichotomous policies, also contributes to resistances (48).

Even though the Iranian regime's ideological hegemony covers vast cultural spheres, Iranian television, more specifically the news programs on Islamic Republic of Iran Broadcasting (IRIB),[6] is the focus of this book. Due to its importance, the translation of the regime's ideological hegemony into IRIB's media policies and structure will be discussed in a separate chapter (Chapter 3), and the success or failure of ideological hegemony in relation to human rights through news dissemination will be explored in Chapters 5–7.

Cultural Counter-Hegemony

Resistances formed in relation to media since the 1979 Islamic Revolution are cultural and spring from the contradictions that exist within the imposed ideological and cultural hegemonies and are evident in both the private and public spheres. Media, as a cultural tool for resistance, could potentially be used for "revolutionary mobilization" (3). Some scholars argue that resistances, in whatever form, are mutually created alongside power. This argument is based on Michel Foucault's work on the relationship between power and resistance. Foucault believed that, wherever power exists, resistance also exists. Because of this significant relation, resistance can never be positioned outside the domain of power (51). To Foucault, power does not mean what one may typically think of it, e.g. as an institution or structure. It is not even about the strength individuals might possess. It is rather a title given to "a complex strategical situation in a particular society" (51). These complex power relations depend on multifaceted resistance, or a "plurality of resistances" (51).

Iranian scholars have identified diverse cultural resistance synapses that developed in Iran as a result of "hegemonic, official Islamic culture" in relation to the rearrangement of the broadcasting system after the Islamic Revolution, the predicaments faced by the Iranian regime in its attempt to create an Islamic television, and the cultural resistance within the society up until 1991 (48). Some scholars believe that the civil society is a platform on which the legitimization of the regime and authoritarianism occurs (47). Thus, despite resistance, the Iranian regime has maintained its position for the past 40 years. The state's imposed position has been the Islamic Republic's stronghold to "maintain legitimacy while being contested in civil society" (52).

Conclusion

Most research involving the application of theories to the case of Iran such as its incomplete transformation and transition of political system in 1979 and the resulting birth of a hybrid authoritarianism, the creation of the concept of *velayat-e faqih*, and Khomeini's imposition of a single religio-cultural identity based on re-traditionalized Shi'ite values seeks to explain the nature of Iran's existence and not how the Iranian regime's ideologies translate themselves into practice. It is, therefore, advantageous to investigate, an undertaking never done before, how the national state television, as one of the regime's most powerful cultural tools, portrays international human rights principles, which the regime has endorsed as being universal by signing the relevant treaties. Television, as one form of contribution to cultural hegemony and power, tends to create resistance. How this looks like and whether it resonates in the case of Iran are also worth investigating. The research on both the television and Iranians fills a wide gap in the literature.

Notes

1 In Shi'i doctrine, the title of "Imam" is reserved "only for the twelve descendants of the Prophet Muhammad." An Imam leads the "ummat" in every religious, spiritual, and political matter.
2 Zinecker defines "rent economy" as the surplus that the state allocates to workers as opposed to the profit earned by the "free business competition" in the market, hence the name "market economy."
3 In order to "strengthen his political base, avoid unrest, and secure continued American support," the Shah introduced a "White Revolution," which included but was not limited to the "continuation of land redistribution from wealthy landlords to landless peasants."
4 UN Watch is a human rights organization that monitors United Nations' compliance with principles of its charter.
5 In Iran, the Mullahs wear white turbans. Black turbans are reserved for those who are direct descendants of Prophet Muhammad.
6 *Seda va Simay-e Jomhouri-e Islamiy-e Iran* translates to *the Voice and Vision of the Islamic Republic (VVIR)*.

References

1. Milani MM. *The making of Iran's Islamic Revolution: From monarchy to Islamic Republic.* 2nd ed. New York & London: Routledge; 1988:1.
2. Arjomand SA. The search for fundamentals and Islamic fundamentalism. In: Vucht Tijssen Lv, Berting J, Lechner F, editors. *The search for fundamentals: The process of modernisation and the quest for meaning.* Dordrecht: Springer; 1995:29–30.
3. Sreberny-Mohammadi A, Mohammadi A. *Small media, big revolution: Communication, culture, and the Iranian Revolution.* Minneapolis & London: University of Minnesota Press; 1994:11.
4. Bayat M. The Iranian Revolution of 1978–79: Fundamentalist or modern? *Middle East Journal.* 1983;37(1):32.
5. Boroumand L, Boroumand R. Illusion and reality of civil society in Iran: An ideological debate. *Social Research: An International Quarterly.* 2000;67(2):202–308.
6. Shari'ati A. *Ummat va Imamat (Community and Leadership).* Ketabnak: Teribon-i Mostazafin; 2012:16 & 19.
7. Afshar H. Khomeini's teachings and their implications for women. *Feminist Review.* 1982;12(1):60.
8. Khomeini R. *Sahifeyeh Imam: Collection of works by Imam Khomeini (Volume 5).* Tehran: The Institute for the Compilation and Publication of the Works of Imam Khomeini; 1999. Available from: http://www.imam-khomeini.ir/fa/C207_41889/رارف_ازا_هاش_ناریا_ـ_تغیراـتیآ_ندها_یناریا20%#page132:133.

9. Khomeini R. *Sahifeyeh Imam: Collection of works by Imam Khomeini (Volume 4)*. Tehran: The Institute for the Compilation and Publication of the Works of Imam Khomeini; 1999. Available from: http://www.imam-khomeini.ir/fa/C207_41803/ع_لت_ترک_عراق_و_مهاجرت_به_فرانسه20% #page244:244.

10. NewYorkTimes. *An interview with Khomeini*. The New York Times; 1979. Available from: https://www.nytimes.com/1979/10/07/archives/an-interview-with-khomeini.html.

11. Khomeini RM. *Quotes from Ayatollah I Khomeini*. Iran Heritage; 2003 [Ayatollah Khomeini (in a meeting with Iranian students and educators, Qom, [3] March 13, 1979)]. Available from: http://www.iran-heritage.org/?page_id=283.

12. Zinecker H. Regime-hybridity in developing countries: Achievements and limitations of new research on transitions. *International Studies Review*. 2009;11(2):303.

13. Lewis D. Civil society and the authoritarian state: Cooperation, contestation and discourse. *Journal of Civil Society*. 2013;9(3):1.

14. Abrahamian E. *Iran between two revolutions*. Princeton, NJ: Princeton University Press; 1982:448 & 427.

15. Summitt AR. For a White Revolution: John F. Kennedy and the Shah of Iran. *Middle East Journal*. 2004;58(4):569.

16. Amuzegar J. The Iranian economy before and after the Revolution. *Middle East Journal*. 1992;46(3):413–4.

17. Mahdavy H. Patterns and problems of economic development in rentier states: The case of Iran. In: Cook MA, editor. *Studies in economic history of the Middle East: From the rise of Islam to the present day*. Oxford: Oxford University Press; 1970:428.

18. Luciani G. Allocation vs. production states: A theoretical framework. In: Luciani G, editor. *The Arab state*. London: Routledge; 1990:71 & 75.

19. Ross ML. Does taxation lead to representation? *British Journal of Political Science*. 2004;34(2):24.

20. Arjomand SA. *After Khomeini: Iran under his successors*. New York & Oxford: Oxford University Press; 2009:122.

21. Gray M. *A theory of "Late Rentierism" in the Arab states of the Gulf*. Occassional Paper. Georgetown University: School of Foreign Service in Qatar, Studies CfIaR; 2011:6.

22. Khiabany G. *Iranian media: The paradox of modernity*. London: Routledge; 2010:43 & 125.

23. Parvin M, Vaziri M. Islamic man and society in the Islamic Republic of Iran. In: Farsoun SK, Mashayekhi M, editors. *Iran: Political culture in the Islamic Republic*. London & New York: Routledge; 1992:81, 86–87 & 90.

24. IRI. *Constitution of the Islamic Republic of Iran*. Foundation for Iranian Studies; 1989. Available from: http://fis-iran.org/en/resources/legaldoc/constitutionislamic.

25. Fukuyama F. Iran, Islam and rule of law. *The Wall Street Journal*. 2009. Available from: https://www.wsj.com/articles/SB10001424052970203946904574300374086282670.

26. Tamadonfar M. Islam, law, and political control in contemporary Iran. *Journal for the Scientific Study of Religion.* 2001;40(2):206.
27. Khiabany G, Sreberny A. The Iranian press and the continuing struggle over civil society 1998–2000. *International Communication Gazette.* 2001;63(2–3):206.
28. Schirazi A. *The Constitution of Iran: Politics and the state in the Islamic Republic.* London: Tauris; 1997:142.
29. Lears TJJ. The concept of cultural hegemony—problems and possibilities. *American Historical Review.* 1985;90(3):568.
30. IRIN. *Iran: Non-election to UN Human Rights Council welcomed by watchdog group.* UN Watch; 2006 [May 22, 2014]. Available from: http://www.unwatch.org/site/c.bdKKISNqEmG/b.1289203/apps/s/content.asp?ct=2453759.
31. Geertz C. *The interpretation of cultures: Selected essays.* New York: Basic Books, Inc., Publishers; 1973:219.
32. Hunt A. *Governing morals: A social history of moral regulation.* Cambridge: Cambridge University Press; 1999:194.
33. Hobsbawm EJ. Introduction: Inventing traditions. In: Hobsbawm EJ, Ranger TO, editors. *The invention of tradition.* Cambridge: Cambridge University Press; 2000:1 & 4.
34. Arjomand SA. Traditionalism in twentieth-century Iran. In: Arjomand SA, editor. *From nationalism to revolutionary Islam.* Albany: State University of New York Press; 1984:196–197.
35. Richter J. *Iran: The culture.* New York: Crabtree Publishing Company; 2005:9.
36. Fischer MMJ. *Mute dreams, blind owls, and dispersed knowledges: Persian poesis in the transnational circuitry.* Durham, NC: Duke University Press; 2004:163.
37. Al-e- Ahmad J. *Occidentosis: A plague from the West (Gharbzadegi).* Berkeley, CA: Mizan Press; 1983. Available from: http://mohsen.1.banan.byname.net/content/republished/doc.public/politics/iran/gharbzadegi/campbellTranslation/Occidentosis-A-Plague-From-the-West.pdf/view.
38. Boroujerdi M. Gharbzadegi: The dominant intellectual discourse of pre- and post-Revolutionary Iran. In: Farsoun SK, Mashayekhi M, editors. *Iran: Political culture in the Islamic Republic.* London & New York: Routledge; 1992:24.
39. Arendt H. Freedom and politics: A lecture. *Chicago Review.* 1960;14(1):35.
40. Schmitt C. The age of neutralizations and depoliticizations (1929). In: Expanded Edition, editor. *Carl Schmitt: The concept of the political.* Chicago, IL: University of Chicago Press; 2007:87.
41. Mouffe C. *Agonistics: Thinking the world politically.* London & New York: Verso; 2013:2–6.
42. Mouffe C. By way of a postscript. *Parallax.* 2014;20(2):150.
43. Schmitt C. The concept of the political (1932). In: Expanded Edition, editor. *Carl Schmitt: The concept of the political.* Chicago, IL: University of Chicago Press; 2007:29–30.

44. Jahanbegloo R. The two sovereignties and the legitimacy crisis in Iran. *Constellations.* 2010;17(1):22.
45. Gramsci A. *Selections from the prison notebooks of Antonio Gramsci.* London: Lawrence and Wishart; 1971:187, 258 & 322.
46. Pratt N. Bringing politics back in: Examining the link between globalization and democratization. *Review of International Political Economy.* 2004;11(2):318.
47. Pratt NC. *Democracy and authoritarianism in the Arab World.* Boulder, CO & London: Lynne Rienner Publishers; 2006:9, 10 & 14.
48. Sreberny-Mohammadi A, Mohammadi A. Hegemony and resistance: Media politics in the Islamic Republic of Iran. *Quarterly Review of Film and Video.* 1991;12(4):33 & 36.
49. Skocpol T. *States and social revolutions: A comparative analysis of France, Russia and China.* Cambridge: Cambridge University Press; 1979:171.
50. BornaNews Agency. *Iran's approach towards human rights is based on Islam, the Constitution and International Obligations* 2014. Available from: http://www.bornanews.ir/Pages/News-234547.aspx.
51. Foucault M. *The history of sexuality: An introduction.* New York: Pantheon Books; 1978:93 & 95–96.
52. Morady F. The power bloc in Iran: A reply to 'The Changing Formations of the Power Bloc in Iran and the Neo-National Bourgeoisie by Hessam Daryani and Nima Nakhae.' *Global Discourse: An Interdisciplinary Journal of Current Affairs and Applied Contemporary Thought.* 2011;2(2):118.

3 IRIB Structure, Policies, and Position on Human Rights

IRIB: An Islamic Anachronism

Several significant milestones, including the 1979 Revolution, contributed to the policies of the Islamic Republic of Iran, especially to its promotion of antagonistic views of "us" versus "them." The revolution reversed the secularization efforts of the Shah due to the ruling clergy's disdain for most of what the West had to offer (1). Khomeini's regime adopted the concept of Westoxication to combat the influence of the West and promote Islamic culture. How the Islamic Republic of Iran chose, predominantly, to define and shape its policies against Westoxication was twofold and cultural. It first focused on the complete annihilation of Western cultural influence. It then sought to replace Western influence with Islamic culture, which in Khomeini's words were considered pure, authentic "Muhammadan Islam" (2) that had been defiled under the Shah (3). This notion of a pure, authentic Muhammadan Islam was immediately codified in a new constitution.

The importance of media in implementing the new state policies is evident in the preamble of the new Iranian Constitution, which states:

> The mass-communication media, radio, and television, must serve the diffusion of Islamic culture in pursuit of the evolutionary course of the Islamic Revolution. To this end, the media should be used as a forum for healthy encounter of different ideas, but they must strictly refrain from diffusion and propagation of destructive and anti-Islamic practices (4).

This attempt to create an Islamic radio and television after the 1979 Revolution was not without contradictions and resistances. These contradictions and resistances are most specifically apparent in the Islamic Republic of Iran Broadcasting (IRIB) since no Qur'anic guidance is available for IRIB's policies and structure. In other words, IRIB is anachronistic under the Islamic Republic.

There are two general cultural policies that the Islamic Republic of Iran has wished to translate into realistic broadcasting strategies. One is Khomeini's "true Islam," which has given divine guidance, an ideological compass to the state and guidelines to assess culture. The other is Khomeini's "neither East nor West" concept, which has rejected any type of influence, political or cultural, from the world's superpowers at the time of the revolution—the United States and the Soviet Union (5). Khomeini's opposition to nationalism also played a major role in the Islamic Republic's policies concerning the Islamicization of television, something most scholars have ignored. Khomeini repeatedly expressed his loathing toward nationalism and nationalists saying, "Nationalism is against Islam.... It is against God's commandment, and it is against the Quran" (6). Despite such clear guidance from the leader of the revolution, the Iranian regime and Khomeini, himself, have slipped national unity and national pride into the propaganda machinery during times of national crisis such as the Iran-Iraq War of the 1980s.

The History of IRIB

The importance of media was understood long before the 1979 Islamic Revolution. The Shah of Iran used the media to reach out to the masses and win their support on his policies. The existing radio (established in 1964) and a single channel, *Television of Iran*, which was a single television channel (established in 1958), in addition to a second network (established in 1966) merged to form the National Iranian Radio and Television (NIRT) by 1971. NIRT grew quickly both institutionally and geographically to a point where it became the second largest broadcasting network in Asia (3). This popularity persuaded even those in poverty to acquire a television set. Once the 1979 Revolution took place, the Iranian people were equipped to receive their Grand Ayatollah. The NIRT's headquarters was taken over by the Islamic supporters of the revolution on February 11, 1979 (3). Previously, Khomeini had stated, "If this radio and television apparatus, which has influence in every home, even in villages, fails to become 100% Islamic, this would mean that Islam has failed to disembark in Iran" (6).

NIRT was transformed after the Islamic Revolution to the IRIB (7). The literal translation of IRIB or *Sazman-e Seda va Sima-ye Jomhuri-ye Eslami-ye Iran* is "The voice and vision of the Islamic Republic of

Iran" (8), which underscored Khomeini's position on the role of media post-revolution. Khomeini singled out television as being of particular importance, stating, "Television is the most sensitive amongst all propaganda issues and apparatuses since it is both the ear and the eye" (9). The majority of Khomeini's views ultimately became IRIB policies.

Khomeini and IRIB

Khomeini wanted to use radio and television as educational tools. That is why IRIB is also considered to be a public university (10). He stated, "This apparatus [IRIB] must be an apparatus which should enlighten all strata of the nation, bring up revolutionaries and thinkers, nurture them to become independent and liberal, get rid of Westoxication and give people independence..." (11). His purpose for making full use of media was to introduce Islam in its "true" and "correct" form not only to the Iranian people but also to the world. He thought this would be more effective than "thousands of cannons and tanks" (6).

Khomeini also believed that for an Islamic republic to materialize in Iran, the mere mention of or vote for the Islamic Republic was not enough. Khomeini believed that the Islamic Republic's intelligence apparatuses, the press, radio, television, offices, all government centers, all national centers, the bazaar, deserts, and factories should be such that whoever enters them should feel Islam, should see the effect of Islam, should see the footsteps of Islam. He felt that everything contrary to Islamic principles and everything against the Islamic Republic must be destroyed (12). Khomeini's views on media became codified in the constitution and additional policies, laws, and regulations enacted over the years strengthened their legal hold.

Aims and Policies of IRIB

The Iranian Constitution starts with a legal introduction to public media. It states,

> The public media (radio-television) must take their place in the process of development of the Islamic revolution and must serve in the propagation of Islamic culture. In this sphere, they must look for opportunities for a healthy exchange of differing ideas and must rigorously refrain from the propagation and encouragement of destructive and anti-Islamic qualities (ideas).

Interestingly, while this statement points to rigorous refrainment from "the propagation and encouragement of destructive and anti-Islamic qualities (ideas)," the section that follows recognizes freedom and human dignity as the central point of the objectives of the principles of this law. The law is also mentioned as creating a path for "development and perfection of man," through the election of "sagacious and devout representatives" and by exercising "active supervision over their work, to participate in the building up of the Islamic society." All these responsibilities fall on the shoulders of the Islamic community as a whole (13). Even though the constitution mentions a few key human rights principles in relation to the role of the media, such as "freedom," "dignity," "debate," and "development of human beings," projection of the Islamic culture and the creation of a pure Islamic society seem to be the regime's main focus (14).

The preamble of *the General Policies and Principles of IRIB Programs*[1] is also of importance since it reveals the Iranian regime's general mentality about news production and distribution. As a part of the role of radio and television, the document emphasizes two important human rights norms—freedom and dignity—for development and perfection. The preamble states:

> The Islamic Revolution of Iran is a determinate link from the chain of divine movements and insurgencies, which throughout history, has safeguarded its continuity in the scene of the battle between the right and the wrong. By taking advantage of all the facilities, the self-centered powers have extended their dark nightmare on the world stage and to maintain their evil domination, they have proceeded with the cultural, mental and economic exploitation of the deprived. In order to transform the values and to drain humans of Godly identity and to alienate Him from self, they have put the newest modes of propagation at their disposal. For long years, our society was under the control of superpowers and their affiliated mercenaries. During this period, their polytheistic values in all cultural, political, artistic, social and economic areas were imposed on our people in such a way that cleansing all their manifestations and effects from within the society, thoughts and public opinions necessitate a widespread and excessive effort and struggle. Recognizing the impacts and consequences of these polytheistic values in all areas and exposing them would cause the shackles and constraints that prevent the human freedom and dignity in the way of development and perfection to break and vanish. These will make way for their replacement with the noble and novel Islamic values.

Our Islamic Revolution, which attained victory by reliance on One God, the Unity of the Word and the blessing from the thoughtful leadership of His Holiness Grand Ayatollah Imam Khomeini on 22 Bahman 1357 [11 February 1979], expresses the fundamental principles of its system in the second article of the Constitution, in which "equity and justice", "independence" and "national solidarity" have been approved in the framework of the Islamic ideological values.

One of the sensitive institutions that plays a determining role in realizing the goals mentioned above is radio and television, which due to its widespread reach and influential power is of exceptional importance. It was this same apparatus that in the previous dependent and colonial regime of this land was the propagandist of the colonial culture and degrading Western system. By expanding its domain of influence, it was about to create a consumerist society with an identity crisis.

By destroying the degraded and decadent tyrannical values and by designing exalted Islamic values, the radio and television in the Islamic Republic system can and must aspire to free the people from evil chains and based on the Imam's wishes, must be turned into an incredibly large university. In executing this delicate task, the Constitution gives the following guidance:

"The mass-communication media, radio, and television, must serve the diffusion of Islamic culture in pursuit of the evolutionary course of the Islamic Revolution. To this end, the media should be used as a forum for the healthy encounter of different ideas, but they must strictly refrain from diffusion and propagation of destructive and anti-Islamic practices" (4).

By disseminating ideological, political and social information, by creating a sense of responsibility in people and by exposing conspiracies and plots of external and internal enemies against the revolution, the Islamic Republic of Iran Broadcasting (IRIB) must strive for its [revolution] protection and sustenance. It must also prepare the grounds for the growth and blossoming of talents and for enhancing people's creativity to the point of Divine Caliphacy. The guiding and prophetic mission of this mass media is the active presence in all social matters and the instilment of the spirit of hope and trust in the society. Besides predicting and warning about the bitter truth and dangers that threaten the community in a timely fashion, it must invite people towards absolute loyalty and excellence. It must also be clear guidance in times of crisis and difficulty.

It is evident that IRIB must never declare itself as the source of all solutions. Instead, by only playing the guiding and informing role, it must lay the foundations of a revolutionary and momentous movement in the context of the Islamic society. To achieve this, people must be informed of all incidents and events as they occur. By benefiting from artistic creativities and fruitful ideas, [IRIB] must focus on culturally, politically, socially, scientifically, technically and artistically educating the people and raising their knowledge and learning standards.

In addition, by presenting the Islamic culture and ideology at the global level, it [IRIB] must materialize the exportation of the revolution. The other mission of this media is addressing the recreational needs of the community and enriching the leisure time of the public through the broadcast of beneficial recreational programs so that the community is secured with a healthy body and soul and a tranquil mind (10).

The earlier preamble illustrates the goal of the Iranian regime to eradicate the effects of the Western culture and replace its satanic values with the elevated values of Islam. These exalted values include "giving" people back their freedom and dignity and releasing them from the earthly and worldly bondage. It aims to put Iranians on a path through which they can spread their wings toward development and perfection. The regime intends to do this by recognizing and then exposing evil influences through the use of radio and television. Of course, the preamble of the UN's Universal Declaration of Human Rights, to which Iran is a signatory, alludes to the "recognition of the inherent dignity" and the "equal and inalienable rights" of everyone to the "foundation of freedom" (15). Hence, these are individual inherent rights, not something that is bestowed or taken away by those in positions of power.

One of the characteristics of the Iranian regime is its wheeling and dealing nature in relation to policies. The earlier preamble is a clear example of one such policy. The Islamic Republic of Iran generously gives nobility back to the people, as nobility is not looked upon as an inherent right of human beings. Freedom has also been given back to the people. The equal and inalienable right of everyone in the world is not recognized as the freedom to choose the kind of values each person wishes to live by. It is rather the only liberating force that should be disseminated throughout the world for global salvation, and IRIB has the critical responsibility of materializing it.

The most significant IRIB policy, as laid out in the Constitution, is highlighted in Article 175. This article is more specific about the type of freedom than what was mentioned in the preamble, stating "The freedom of expression and dissemination of thoughts in the Radio and Television of the Islamic Republic of Iran must be guaranteed." However, this freedom is limited to "the Islamic criteria and the best interests of the country." There is no clear definition of what the Islamic criteria and the interests of the country are. This article also lays out the general structure of IRIB:

> The appointment and dismissal of the head of the Radio and Television of the Islamic Republic of Iran rest with the Leader. A council consisting of two representatives each of the President, the head of the judiciary branch and the Islamic Consultative Assembly shall supervise the functioning of this organization. The policies and the manner of managing the organization and its supervision will be determined by law (4).

The appointment and dismissal of the head of IRIB are left to the Supreme Leader. This power is given in spite of other statements by Khomeini such as

> we must give value and independence to people. We must step aside and just control against good and evil. But it is not right to have everything in our control. It is not right to have radio and television in our control while these poor souls who do all the work have nothing in their control. It is not right for us, who have no role, to have all the control (9).

Given this administrative law and Khomeini's words, it is incumbent to examine IRIB's general administrative structure in connection with the state.

IRIB Administration in Relation to the State

Based on Article 175 and following the approval of its implementation (16), the Supervision Council of IRIB was formed. This council became formally established on October 3, 1991. It is constituted of representatives of the three branches of the government. By 2014, the number of representatives on the Supervision Council grew to 39: 16 from the legislative branch, 11 from the executive branch, and 12 from the judicial branch (17). Among the names of representatives on the Supervision Council, one, in particular, stands out: Mohammad-Javad Larijani. Larijani was, and still is, the Head of the High Council for Human Rights of the Islamic Republic of Iran (18). One of his brothers, Ali Larijani, was, and still is, the current chairman of the Parliament. Another brother, Sadeq Larijani, is the current head of judiciary (19).

Under the rules established for IRIB, all radio (voice) and television (vision) programs are recorded and monitored by "experts" in five managerial groups: television supervision, radio supervision, supervision on executive procedures, supervision on political and news programs, managing supervision on technical matters, and social media of the council. The experts of the council put forth any issues that may arise from weekly meetings of representatives of the three branches of the judiciary (17).

In theory, based on Article 175, the head of IRIB reports to the Supervision Council. However, he is ultimately responsible for answering to the Supreme Leader, who based on Article 110 (paragraph 6.3) of the Constitution appoints, dismisses, and accepts resignations from "the head of the radio and television network of the Islamic Republic of Iran" (4).

At the end of Akbar Hashemi Rafsanjani's presidency (1989–1997) and during the presidency of Mohammad Khatami (1997–2005), there was an attempt by the Office of the Supreme Leader to gain more control over the cultural atmosphere of the country. During this time a new face emerged among the personnel of the Supreme Leader's Office. His name is Hossein Mohammadi, and he has turned into the most powerful person in influencing, delivering, and executing cultural policies in Iran today. From the Supreme Leader's Office, Mohammadi went on to work at IRIB and during Ali Larijani's role as the head of IRIB, Mohammadi became the deputy to the Political Affairs Department. He then returned to the Supreme Leader's Office and continued his activities there. Mohammadi is responsible for some of the most important news bulletins and news broadcast from Iran's radio and television as well as being responsible for setting and communicating the news policies of IRIB. He plays a key role in the Supreme Leader's meetings with cultural experts in addition to arranging private meetings between journalists and authors and the Supreme Leader. Mohammadi is not a member of the Supreme Council of the Cultural Revolution, but he plays a crucial role in communicating the cultural policies of the Supreme Leader's Office to this institution (20).

Decisions and policies concerning media are, therefore, always regulated through the Supreme Leader even though there are seemingly checks and balances. Figure 3.1 shows the general structure of IRIB in connection with the state and in relation to the Supreme Leader (8).

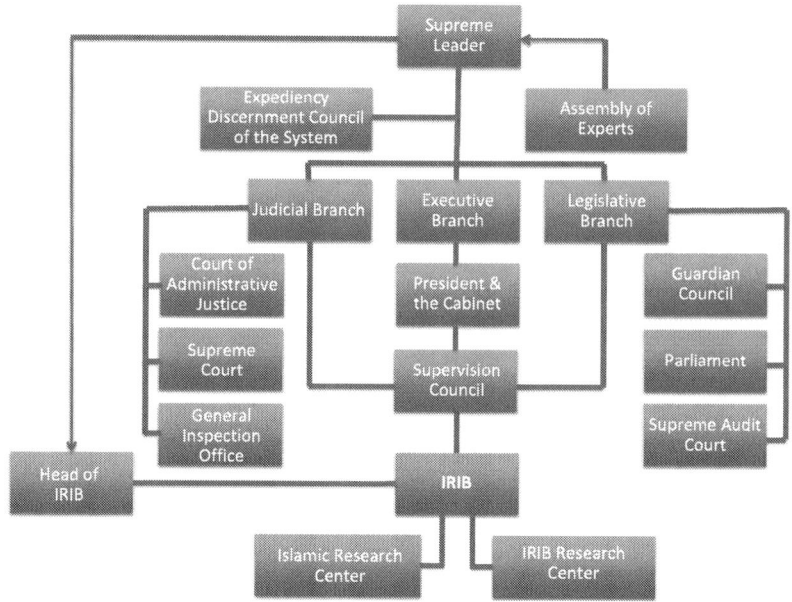

Figure 3.1 The general administrative structure of IRIB in relation to the state.

IRIB Organization

IRIB is a very complicated organization. Table 3.1 illustrates a general and simple setup of IRIB according to Tebyan Cultural and Information Center affiliated with the Islamic Development Organization (21).

Based on *IRIB's Public Relations*, published on The Center of Art & Cultural Education website (Applied Science & Technology University Unit 13), the administrative system of IRIB looks a little different from Table 3.1 (22). Figure 3.2 shows the various divisions and units of this organization according to IRIB's Public Relations' publication.

Even though all units in IRIB are intertwined with and influenced by each other, the focus of this book is on one particular unit whose function is to provide news material for all local, national, and overseas radio and television channels except for *Al-Alam*, *Al-Kowthar*, *Sahar TV*, and *Press TV* channels. This unit called the Central News Unit, or *Vahedeh Markazieh Khabar*, is nested under the Political Affairs Department (Figure 3.2). Based on Article 20(B) of *The Article*

Table 3.1 The General Setup of the IRIB Organization

Setup of the IRIB Organization

1	Headquarter Division	a The Research and Programming Department
		b Presidential District
		c Parliament and Provinces Affairs Department
		d Security Management
		e International Communications Affairs Department
		f Human Resources
2	Supporting Division	a The Financial and Administrative Department
		b Education Department
		c Technical Operations Department
		d The Planning and Expansion Department
3	Execution Division	a Voice Department
		b Vision Department
		c Political Affairs Department
		d Foreign Affairs Department
		e Total Voice and Vision Offices for Provinces and Counties
		f Representative Offices Outside the Country
		g Choir and Music Centre

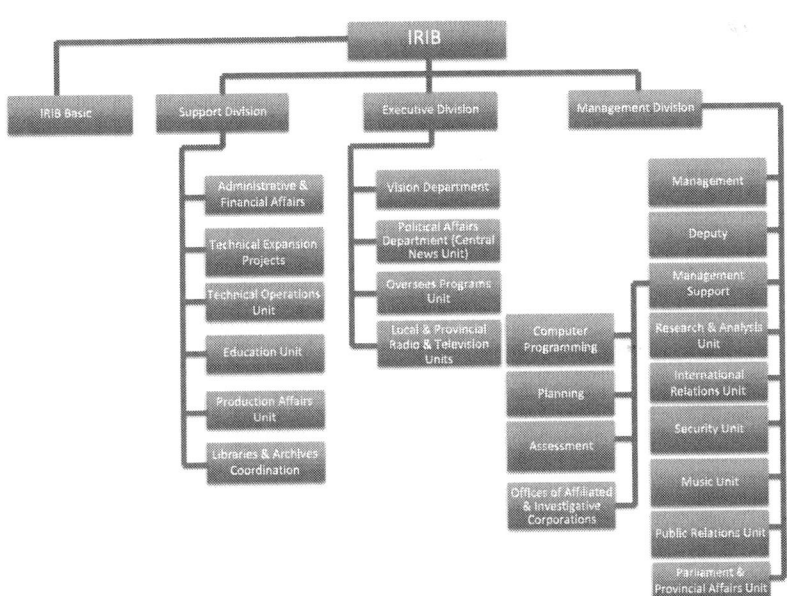

Figure 3.2 IRIB setup based on The Center of Art & Cultural Education's publication.

of Association (statute) of IRIB, the Political Affairs Department should assist the Supervision Council in "defining and formulating the ad hoc policies for news, commentaries, and political programming and overseeing their implementation" (23). In addition, according to Article 21(2), the deputy of Political Affairs is "responsible for production, editing, and broadcasting of news, reports, commentaries and political analyses. The department receives all its news policies from the Political Bureaus" (23). The Central News Unit, in turn, provides and distributes the news to other channels in various areas such as politics, economics, social, scientific, cultural, arts, and sports (24).

Even though the Central News Unit is responsible for news production and distribution, the head of IRIB is accountable for all programming decisions. In a decree dated November 6, 2014, Khamenei appointed Mohammad Sarafraz as the new head of IRIB. Sarafraz replaced Ezzatollah Zarghami who was the head of IRIB for ten years (25). Khamenei appointed Zarghami on May 23, 2004, in Ali Larijani's place as the head of IRIB. Zarghami was Larijani's deputy during his tenure (26). Interestingly, The Council of the European Union has blacklisted both Zarghami (27) and Sarafraz (28) as violators of international provisions on due process and fair trial. As heads of IRIB responsible for all programming decisions, they had "worked with the Iranian security services and prosecutors to broadcast forced confessions of detainees" (28).

Following Sarafraz's appointment, a few changes were made to IRIB organization. One of the noteworthy changes was targeted toward the Central News Unit, which changed its name to *Khabargozarieh Seda va Sima* (IRIB News Agency) in December 2015 (29, 30). Mehrdad Seyed Mehdi was also chosen as the new head of this unit. In addition to paying serious attention to components such as speed and accuracy in the production of the news, he was requested to focus on issues such as news productions, connecting with overseas radio and television networks, increasing the quality of incoming reports, and strengthening the quality of news content and images (29). This request was made by IRIB's new Political Deputy, Peyman Jebeli (31).

IRIB and News Policy

While there is a complicated structural system within IRIB, a study carried out by Arbatani et al. from the University of Tehran on *Challenges of News Policy in the Islamic Republic of Iran Broadcasting (IRIB): A Qualitative Study*, where 19 "experts and specialists in the field of news and news policy" and "directors of IRIB" were interviewed, shows that the general policymaking of IRIB news is influenced by five different entities. First and foremost are the "intentions" of the Supreme Leader "in relation to the duties and responsibilities of the national media" (32). Any statement by the Supreme Leader regarding state media is placed on the agenda of the organization and ends up as a policy of IRIB. Such policies, however, may or may not be fully implemented. Nonetheless, since the head of IRIB is appointed and dismissed by the Supreme Leader, his statements carry a great deal of weight.

The second influential set of elements that affect IRIB policies is the general codifications that set out IRIB's responsibilities toward various issues within the nation. Such codifications lay the foundation for any future policies within IRIB. One such codification is laid out in Article 175 of the Iranian Constitution, for instance. After Khomeini's death in 1989, Article 175 was amended[2] (33), including a few changes that Khomeini had wished to make toward the end of his life. The eight-year Iran-Iraq War (1980–1988), which started almost immediately after the 1979 Islamic Revolution, postponed earlier changes to the constitution. Soon after Khomeini's death, Rafsanjani, a member of the Constitutional Review Council Khomeini had created to oversee the amendments and modifications of the constitution, was elected president. The revisions were approved by the Supreme Leader first and then put to a national vote a week later. This referendum coincided with the presidential election. Therefore, it was during Rafsanjani's presidency that the constitutional changes were approved and implemented.

The third element that has affected the IRIB policies since the 1979 Revolution is the agenda of various governments that have come to power. As one of the most potent tools of propaganda, especially during sensitive periods such as elections, IRIB has been used by various governments to sway public opinion through the dissemination of propaganda for the benefit of the ruling party. They achieve this through the involvement of the IRIB Policy Council (Supervision Council), comprised of the members of the executive, legislative, and judiciary branches of government. The fourth element affecting IRIB policies, according to Arbatani et al., is the attitude that political parties take toward various candidates, using IRIB for such purposes. This attitude has, of course, more demonstrable bearing in times of presidential elections. However, the use of IRIB as a propaganda machine by various state agencies is not limited to such periods since those involved with this state-owned and state-controlled media are themselves affiliated with various political parties. Finally, IRIB's battle with the external media to attract and maintain audience also influences the nature of policy within IRIB (32). Even though the Iranian Constitution has been revised only once since the establishment of the Islamic Republic, various laws and regulations have been added consistently to its different articles. Article 175 is no exception.

IRIB Policies

Parliament approved *The Article of Association (statute) of IRIB* on October 19, 1983 (34). Article 9 of this document articulates the central objective of IRIB:

> The main objective[s] of the organization as a popular [public] university is [are] promotion of Islamic culture, creation of suitable condition for purification, education of people and enhancement of moral values, and expediting the evolutionary process of the Islamic Revolution across the world. These objectives should be attained within the framework of entertainment, educational, guidelines, news, and recreational programs (23).

A separate document, *the General Policies and Principles of IRIB Programs*, approved by Parliament on July 8, 1982, further lays out IRIB's goals (35). Article 1 of Section 1 (general principles) establishes the policy of "the dominance of Islamic views in all programs and avoidance of broadcasting programs contrary to Islamic standards."

Concerning news coverage, Article 16 states, "IRIB, through continuous presence in the society, should always reflect the important events of the country fairly and inform the people about the truth." This policy is complemented by Article 17, which states, "IRIB should reflect the events, activities, and problems of the whole country based on the regional priorities and in a fair manner in its national channels." While Article 16 ensures that important social events and incidents get reported as they happen, Article 17 confines it to regional priorities. Therefore, what is deemed important and of priority is ultimately determined by the authorities in charge of IRIB.

Article 18 states that "IRIB is obliged to broadcast the latest accurate news and information about the important local and international events and developments that are useful and interesting to the majority of people in a clear and brief manner." Articles 18 also says that the station is obligated to air what is "useful" and "interesting" to the majority of people; yet the media is entirely controlled by the state, and the public has no say in media policy-making or news production.

Article 19 mandates, "In all programs and news, in particular, issues containing the following items should not be broadcast":

A   Military, economic, and political secrets of the country or items that could be used by the enemy, if revealed.

B   Making false and libel statements against official establishments and institutions, groups, political parties, and associations whose activities are authorized by the law.

C   Issues whose publication would bring moral corruption and indecency to the society as stated in the holy verse "Lo! Those who love that slander be spread concerning those who believe ..."

D   Publication of items, which may undermine the religious feelings and national unity and may cause turmoil in the country.

E   Any item that might be considered propaganda for the counter-revolutionaries and mischievous groups.

F   Any topic that might be considered harmful to the friendly relationship with ally and brother countries or that may undermine and harm the country's foreign relations.

Under Article 19, the newsworthiness of an issue is based on the exclusion of six major but ambiguous areas. The principle of journalistic objectivity is hence completely ignored. The details of Article 19 suggest censorship of news content, elimination of certain information, and partiality over others.

Finally, Article 20 holds that efforts must be "aimed at gathering and obtaining reliable and correct international news and becoming free from the monopoly of the Zionist and imperialist international new[s] agencies" (36). In line with that, Article 27 of Section 4 (cultural programs) maintains that efforts must be aimed at "replacing the eastern and western value systems with the Islamic value system and campaigning against the remnants of the ideas and works of the corrupt culture of the former regime." This article speaks specifically to the worries of Iran's leaders that IRIB's collaboration in the form of shared news footage with international broadcasters such as CNN, Reuters, and the BBC World Service might result in IRIB using footage that casts the Islamic Republic in something other than a positive light (3).

Other policies affecting the IRIB are important since they emphasize the role of media in penetrating people's minds and influencing their behavior. Article 48, for example, states, "IRIB is duty-bound to enhance public intellectual and moral awareness and to pave the way for full implementation of the country's Constitution, which outlines the principles of the Islamic Republic of Iran." Article 50 states, "Efforts [should be] aimed at presenting political and ideological visions to people and increasing their knowledge and awareness about the position of the arrogant world and the oppressed nations." Article 51 belies any pretense to neutrality by IRIB by emphasizing the need for the media to present "the Islamic identity and anti-imperialism characteristics of [the] Iranian nation and revealing the efforts made by the enemy to change such identity and sentiments." Finally, Article 52 obliges IRIB to inform "the people about the evil plots of the world colonial powers and their local agents aimed at weakening or changing the true path of the Revolution" (36). The policies go on to categorize different states and their governments and how IRIB should portray and deal with each of them.

Criticism of the IRIB and Viewer Decline

Under these general policies, IRIB's viewership drastically declined (37). In 2009, Channel 1 had 78% viewership, and it got to its lowest in 2014 (58.6%) (38). As a survival mechanism and in response to the goals set in the policies as mentioned earlier, the number of channels increased, and the number of programs skyrocketed. When Zarghami took office in 2004, there were only seven national television channels, eight national radio channels, 30 provincial radio channels, four provincial television channels, and seven global channels. By 2011, IRIB's global, national, and provincial channels reached 100 (39). During Zarghami's tenure, there was a 72% increase in news reports on television and the launch of 16 multimedia news bases (40). However, even with such proliferation, IRIB was faced with criticism regarding the content of its programs. Akbar Hashemi Rafsanjani, who was the fourth president of Iran[3] and chairman of the Expediency Council, criticized IRIB saying, "There are too many signs of discord broadcast from IRIB these days. We feed people with things that do not exist. These discordances do not serve the country and the revolution" (41).

IRIB was and is expected to cooperate with the Ministry of Culture and Islamic Guidance, which has the duty of promoting and enhancing the "values of the Islamic Revolution based on the school of thought and political outlook of the late Imam Khomeini and the Supreme Leader of the Islamic Revolution" (42). The Ministry is responsible for

> [i]ntroducing the fundamentals, characteristics and objectives of the Islamic Revolution to people of the world by making use of audio-visual media, books and other publications, organizing

cultural gatherings and other events within the country and abroad through coordination with the Ministry of Foreign Affairs and other relevant organizations (Article 2.1).

It is also responsible for

> [c]ollecting news, reports, articles and pictures about Iran and other countries and distributing them among the mass media of the country as well as disseminating and deflecting various events of the country and the region about the political, economic, social, cultural and sport among the news outlets of world countries (Article 2.10) (42).

Even a partial look at the structure and policies of IRIB gives a glimpse of its complex nature. Since this book focuses on IRIB's portrayal of international human rights and humanitarian norms, it is necessary to look at the international human rights principles that have made their way into the IRIB policies.

IRIB Policies on International Human Rights Law

Drawing on Iran's commitment to the international human rights treaties, a few IRIB policies have been based on some of the general principles laid out in the relevant conventions and declarations. However, both the head of IRIB and the Vice-President of Legal Affairs have made it clear that "the mentions of conventions and agreements do not necessarily mean that they are credible or suited for implementation. Their suitability based on credibility and quality is rather left to the relevant authorities" (10). Below are IRIB laws and regulations that are solely based on international core conventions signed and ratified by the Islamic Republic of Iran.

The Convention on the Rights of Persons with Disabilities

A law entitled "Approval of the Convention on the Rights of Persons with Disabilities" was passed on December 3, 2008 (10). Article 2 of the legislation defines some of the key terms used in the convention and terms such as "communication," "language," "discrimination on the basis of disability," "reasonable accommodation," and "universal design" have been included verbatim in IRIB laws and regulations. In addition, Article 8 on "Awareness-raising" is also included. This article obliges signatory states to "foster respect for the rights and dignity of persons with disabilities," to "combat stereotypes, prejudices, and harmful practices relating to persons with disabilities," and to "promote awareness of the capabilities and contributions of persons with disabilities." Finally, Article 21 of this convention is also included in IRIB laws and regulations. Article 21 on the freedom of expression and opinion and access to information gives persons with disabilities the right to express themselves, "including the freedom to seek, receive and impart information and ideas on an equal basis with others and through all forms of communication of their choice." These forms of communication include "the use of sign languages, Braille, augmentative and alternative communication, and all other accessible means, modes, and formats of communication." Mass media, including providers of information through the Internet, is also encouraged to make its services accessible to persons with disabilities.

Inclusion of parts of this convention into IRIB policies is significant since the Islamic Republic of Iran has made the following reservations to the convention: "… with regard to Article 46,[4] the Islamic Republic of Iran declares that it does not consider itself bound by any provisions of the Convention, which may be incompatible with its applicable rules." Because Iran has reservations on the Convention on the Rights of Persons with Disabilities (CRPD), the inclusion of these articles in IRIB policies is meaningless.

The Convention on the Rights of the Child

On February 20, 1994, the *Majlis* (Parliament) also passed a piece of legislation entitled "The law allowing ratification of the Convention on the Rights of the Child." Articles 1, 13, 17, and 29 of this convention are incorporated verbatim into IRIB's laws and regulations. These articles include the definition of the child, freedom of expression, access to information, mass media, and goals of education. On January 4, 2012, the cabinet ministers also approved another law entitled "The By-law of the National Body on the Convention on the Rights of the Child[5]" (43). Articles 1, 2, and 4 of this law also have been incorporated into IRIB policies, and since no English translation exists, they are included in full below:

> Article 1: In this by-law, the following relevant definitions of terms and terminologies will be used.
> Article 1(A): Child: All individuals under 18.
> Article 1(B): Executive organization: Organizations related to the subject matter of Article 5 concerning the laws of the country's civil service management approved in 2008.

Article 1(C): National Body: The National Body on the Convention on the Rights of the Child, which is under decree No. 105847/ t43855h of the Ministry of Justice dated January 10, 2010.

Article 2: Duties and jurisdictions of the National Body are as follows:

Article 2(J): Consistent and multidimensional dissemination of information and raising awareness on issues related to the rights of the child in collaboration with the Ministry of Education, the Islamic Republic of Iran Broadcasting and other mass media.

Article 4: In order to coordinate and to obtain the views of the relevant executive organizations in undertaking tasks and taking actions on subject matters of this by-law, a coordinating council with the membership of the following groups is established:

Article 4(J): one person from the following organizations introduced on an individual basis by executive order or the highest authority:

...

11. The Islamic Republic of Iran Broadcasting (10).

Once again, the inclusion of some of the principles of the Convention on the Rights of the Child (CRC) into IRIB policies and the formation of a monitoring body, while plausible, are subject to reservations by the Islamic Republic of Iran. Upon signature, Iran made a reservation "to the articles and provisions which may be contrary to the Islamic Shariah, and preserve[d] the right to make such particular declaration, upon its ratification." Subsequently, upon ratification, the Iranian Government reserved "the right not to apply any provisions or articles of the Convention that are incompatible with Islamic Laws and the International legislation in effect."

Since Iran's reservations have only been made to CRC and CRPD, it is curious that only the principles of these two conventions have been incorporated into IRIB laws. The other three core conventions are not directly reflected in any IRIB policies and regulations because they are not subject to any reservation and once implemented cannot legally be derogated from.

Conclusion

Following Khomeini's death and with the introduction of the Internet and satellite TV in Iran in the 1990s, IRIB has faced a worrying loss of audience. To that end, it has injected state funding into the organization and has continuously introduced and applied innovative policies into its programs. The extent of competition over audience attraction has been such that IRIB has turned into "a confused and contradictory organization." It was initially established to destroy any cultural influence of the West "through the dissemination of nationally produced, religiously infused television programming." However, it has gradually been "transformed into that which it has sworn to oppose" (44). This contradiction is a clear example of an expression of hybridity in the form of ambiguity and dichotomy. As mentioned previously, since media did not exist at the time the Quran was revealed, there are no Islamic laws on media and how it is supposed to function. Hence, "[w]hat has been offered is made-up law in the interest of the Islamic Republic" (14). Consequently, IRIB has mushroomed and turned into a complicated structure in an attempt to improve its performance. Considering how articles from international treaties have selectively found their way into IRIB policies, this book aims to rigorously analyze the news content produced by IRIB to deduce how the international human rights principles that Iran is committed to are outputted.

Notes

1 *Ghanooneh khateh mash'ieh koli va osouleh barnameh-hayeh sazmaneh seda va simayeh jomhourieh eslamieh Iran.*
2 The 1979 version of Article 175 stated: In the mass media (radio and television), freedom of press and advertisement must be granted in accordance with the Islamic criteria. The media is administered under the joint supervision of the three powers: the judiciary (the Supreme Judicial Council), legislature, and executive. The law determines how this is to take place.
3 A former president of Iran from 1989 to 1997.
4 Article 46—Reservations: (1) Reservations incompatible with the object and purpose of the present Convention shall not be permitted. (2) Reservations may be withdrawn at any time.
5 The National Body on the Convention on the Rights of the Child is a national child rights monitoring body.

References

1. Menashri D. *Post-revolutionary politics in Iran: Religion, society, and power.* London: Frank Cass; 2001:1.
2. Kamrava M. Khomeini and the West. In: Adib-Moghaddam A, editor. *A critical introduction to Khomeini.* New York: Cambridge University Press; 2014:161.
3. Khiabany G. *Iranian media: The paradox of modernity.* London: Routledge; 2010:139, 161–3 & 176.

4. IRI. *Constitution of the Islamic Republic of Iran*. Foundation for Iranian Studies; 1989. Available from: http://fis-iran.org/en/resources/legaldoc/constitutionislamic.

5. Sreberny-Mohammadi A, Mohammadi A. Hegemony and resistance: Media politics in the Islamic Republic of Iran. *Quarterly Review of Film and Video*. 1991;12(4):39.

6. Khomeini R. *Sahifeyeh Imam: Collection of works by Imam Khomeini (Volume 18)*. Tehran: The Institute for the Compilation and Publication of the Works of Imam Khomeini; 1999. Available from: http://www.imam-khomeini.ir/fa/c207_51285/صحیفه_امام/مامام_جدلد_18/صحیفه_امام_-_ج_دل_18.

7. Pahlavi P. Understanding Iran's media diplomacy. *Israel Journal of foreign Affairs*. 2012;VI(2):22.

8. OSC. *Structure of Iran's state-run TV (IRIB)*. Open Source Center; December 16, 2009. Available from: http://fas.org/irp/dni/osc/iran-tv.pdf.

9. Khomeini R. *Sahifeyeh Imam: Collection of works by Imam Khomeini (Volume 19)*. Tehran: The Institute for the Compilation and Publication of the Works of Imam Khomeini; 1999. Available from: http://www.imam-khomeini.ir/fa/c207_51324/صحیفه_امام/مامام_جدلد_19/صحیفه_امام_-_ج_دل_19.

10. Department of Compilation Codification and Publication of Laws and Regulations. *Collection of laws and regulations: Islamic Republic of Iran Broadcasting*. Tehran: Publication and Printing Office; 2015:5, 7, 108, 306–7 & 427.

11. Khomeini R. *Sahifeyeh Imam: Collection of works by Imam Khomeini (Volume 6)*. Tehran: The Institute for the Compilation and Publication of the Works of Imam Khomeini; 1999. Available from: http://www.imam-khomeini.ir/fa/c207_51237/صحیفه_امام/مامام_جدلد_6/صحیفه_امام_-_ج_دل_6.

12. Khomeini R. *Sahifeyeh Imam: Collection of works by Imam Khomeini (Volume 11)*. Tehran: The Institute for the Compilation and Publication of the Works of Imam Khomeini; 1999. Available from: http://www.imam-khomeini.ir/fa/c207_51254/صحیفه_امام/مامام_جدلد_11/صحیفه__امام_-_ج_دل_11:195–196.

13. IRI. *The Constitution of Islamic Republic of Iran*; 1979. Available from: http://www.iranchamber.com/government/laws/constitution.php.

14. Sreberny A, Khiabany G. *Blogistan: The Internet and politics in Iran*. London: I. B. Tauris; 2010.

15. UN. *The Universal Declaration of Human Rights*. United Nations General Assembly, editor: [Lake Success]; 1948:63–4 & 85.

16. Rafsanjani AH. *The implementation method of Article 175 of the Constitution in Supervision Section*; 3 October 1991. Available from: http://64040.ir/fa/forms/15.

17. Supervision Council. *About the Supervision Council over Islamic Republic of Iran Broadcasting*; 2015. Available from: http://64040.ir/fa/forms/11.

18. UN General Assembly. Situation of human rights in the Islamic Republic of Iran (A/69/306). 12 August 2014. Contract No.: A/69/306.

19. Katzman K. *Iran, Gulf security, and U.S. policy*. Congressional Research Service; 2015. Available from: http://www.fas.org/sgp/crs/mideast/RL32048.pdf:13.
20. BBC Persian. *Ayatollah Khamenei's men*; 2011. Available from: http://www.bbc.com/persian/iran/2011/09/110916_l13_khamenei_men.shtml.
21. Tebyan. *Familiarization with IRIB Organization*; May 12, 2012. Available from: http://www.tebyan.net/newindex.aspx?pid=934&articleID=709034.
22. Toustani AK. *IRIB public relations*. The Center of Art & Cultural Education: Applied Science & Technology University Unit 13; June 9, 2013. Available from: http://www.uast13.ir/مجموعه-ه-های-فارسی/77-درواه- روم-ا-شی ای ارگ-ی موم ع-طباور-ی نی براک/ای نی براک/ا-هف رح-ی سانشراک/ای تراهم رساهن/4722-اورباط-ع مومی-سامزان-صداو-سیامی-ج-ا-ا؟lang=fa.
23. IHRDC. *The Article of Association (statute) of IRIB*. New Haven, CT: Iran Human Rights Documentation Center; 2009. Available from: http://www.iranhrdc.org/english/human-rights-documents/iranian-codes/3356-the-article-of-association-statute-of-irib.html.
24. IRIBNews. *Central News Unit*; 2015. Available from: http://www.irib news.ir/.
25. Khamenei A. *Appointment of Mr. Mohammad Sarafraz as the head of IRIB*; November 8, 2014. Available from: http://farsi.khamenei.ir/message-content?id=28138.
26. Iranian Journalists. *From Ghotbzadeh to Zarghami: IRIB highlights in the span of 36 years*; November 27, 2014. Available from: http://khabarnega ran.info/article.php3?id_article=4176.
27. European Union. *Council decision 2012/168/CFSP*; March 23, 2012. Available from: http://eur-lex.europa.eu/LexUriServ/LexUriServ.do?uri=OJ: L:2012:087:0085:0089:EN:PDF.
28. European Union. *Council implementing regulation (EU) No 206/2013*; March 11, 2013. Available from: http://eur-lex.europa.eu/legal-content/EN/TXT/HTML/?uri=CELEX:32013R0206&qid=1415463734874&from=EN.
29. Asr Iran. *Name change of "Central News Unit" to "IRIB News Agency"*; March 1, 2015. Available from: https://www.asriran.com/fa/news/384994/ ییی ر-نام-وحاد-مرکزی-رب-هب-هخ-رب-رازگی-صداوسیما.
30. IRIB News Agency. *About us*. IRIB News: IRIB News Agency; 2015. Available from: http://www.iribnews.ir/fa/about.
31. Entekhab. *"Jebeli" becomes IRIB's Political Deputy*; January 5, 2015. Available from: http://www.entekhab.ir/fa/news/183867.
32. Arbatani TR, Labafi S, Omidi A. Challenges of news policy in the Islamic Republic of Iran Broadcasting (IRIB): A qualitative study. *International Journal of Academic Research in Accounting, Finance and Management Sciences*. 2016;6(2):188–90.
33. Papan-Matin F (trans.). The Constitution of the Islamic Republic of Iran (1989 Edition). *Iranian Studies*. 2014;47(1):199.
34. Hashemi A. *The Article of Association (statute) of IRIB*; 1983. Available from: http://rc.majlis.ir/fa/law/show/90402.

35. Hashemi A. *The general policies and principles of IRIB programs*. Islamic Parliament Research Center; 1982. Available from: http://rc.majlis.ir/fa/law/show/90575.

36. IHRDC. *General policies and principles of the programs of the Organization IRIB*; 1982. Available from: http://www.iranhrdc.org/english/human-rights-documents/iranian-codes/3355-general-policies-and-principles-of-the-programs-of-the-organization-irib-islamic-republic-of-iran-broadcasting-irib.html.

37. Radio Farda. *IRIB: From Zarghami to Sarafraz*; 2014. Available from: http://www.radiofarda.com/content/f3-feature-on-iran-tv-managment/26680070.html.

38. Rouydad24. *Admittance of television to the fall of viewership after 2009*. Rouydad24; 2016. Available from: https://www.rouydad24.ir/fa/news/14815/اعتراف-تلویزیون-به-ریزش-مخاطب-بعد-از-سال-88.

39. Tabnak. *The number of IRIB's channels reached a hundred*; August 16, 2011. Available from: https://www.tabnak.ir/fa/news/184186/تعداد-شبکه-های-صدا-و-سیما-به-100-رسید.

40. Dana. *A look at Zarghami's ten year management of IRIB*; October 28, 2014. Available from: http://www.dana.ir/News/162102.html.

41. BBC Persian. *Hashemi Rafsanjani: There are signs of discord broadcast from IRIB*; January 1, 2015. Available from: http://www.bbc.co.uk/persian/iran/2015/01/150101_hashemi_rafsanjani?ocid=socialflow_facebook.

42. The Ministry of Culture & Islamic Guidance. *Laws on objectives and responsibilities of the Ministry of Culture & Islamic Guidance*; 1987. Available from: http://www.farhang.gov.ir/en/profileofministry/responsibilities.

43. UNICEF. *UNICEF annual report 2012 for Iran*; 2012. Available from: http://www.unicef.org/about/annualreport/files/Iran_COAR_2012.pdf:2.

44. Marchant J. The revolution will be televised: State and satellite TV in Iran. In: Robertson B, Marchant J, editors. *Revolution decoded: Iran's digital media landscape*. London: Small Media; 2014:64.

4 Quantitative Analysis of the Iranian Television News Programs

From State Obligation to Implementation

As a UN member, Iran is obliged to obey the international human rights law. Under this law, states are obliged to respect, to protect, and to fulfill human rights (1). Once a member, a state also assumes the obligation to remedy human rights violations if and when they occur. At the same time, states are obliged to promote human rights culture and raise awareness of human rights principles. The latter aspect of Iran's obligation as a state is hardly ever scrutinized. This chapter analyzes Iranian news using content analysis (CA). In 2011, Iran informed the UN that "[m]easures had been taken to create a culture of human rights awareness, including the dissemination of interviews and information in the media...."[1] This chapter and the following two chapters are aimed at examining this claim.

Content Analysis

An exploratory approach was taken toward a randomly selected month of the primetime news program on IRIB Channel 1 in the summer of 2014. Eight categories were chosen as variables based on international human rights principles, customary norms, and *jus cogens*. Besides the eight categories, seven human rights terms were chosen as variables for analysis. Unless otherwise stated, the percentages presented in this chapter are the sum of the total mentions of each term or category over the total mentions of all international human rights terms and categories. Table 4.1 shows the 15 categories and terms that were used as variables in the analysis.

Human Rights Coverage in the News

Of all the variables that were assessed, the "right to life" had the highest coverage in the news. "Right to life" was mentioned 16% of the time.

Table 4.1 Fifteen Categories and Terms Used as Variables for Analysis

Categories	Terms
Right to Life	Islamic Human Rights
Right to Freedom from Genocide	Human Rights Violation
Right to Freedom from Discrimination	Human Rights
Right to Political Participation	Rights
Right to Freedom of Expression and Association	Humanitarian Aid
Right to Freedom of Assembly	United Nations
Protection of Civilians	International norms or standards
Right to Protection of Journalists in Conflict	

The "right to freedom of expression and association" followed with 15% coverage in the news. The "right to freedom of assembly," the "protection of civilians," and "the right to freedom from genocide" garnered 15%, 14%, and 12% coverage, respectively. The other variables such as the "United Nations," "humanitarian aid," "rights," "human rights," the "right to freedom from discrimination," the "right to political participation," and the "right to protection of journalists in conflict" had between 1% to 10% coverage in the news. Finally, the "Islamic human rights," "human rights violation," and the "international norms and standards" had less than 1% coverage in the news. Several categorical variables included more than one term; for example, the "right to life" included the terms "killed," "martyred," "lost lives," "death," "murder," and "execution."[2]

Prior to the start of research, it was hard to hypothesize or form a preconceived opinion on what may be the result. The hybrid nature of the Islamic Republic makes predictions difficult. The Islamic Republic had stated to the UN that it had taken measures to create a "culture of human rights awareness" in the media, so it was possible that they had done so to some extent to make a case with the UN. However, considering the bleak human rights record of the Islamic Republic of Iran, it is surprising to find any mention of human rights at all. It is also curious that only certain human rights principles are mentioned and not others. Here is where the context in which the human rights categories and terms get mentioned becomes important. All news packages, in which any mention of human rights terms or categories was made, were therefore contextualized.

The contexts surrounding the coverage of the principles of international human rights, humanitarian law, and *jus cogens* were mostly either political or regarding armed conflict. Other crucial contexts such as ethical, social, cultural, and religious, which are equally relevant to international human rights law and which are the focus of the International Bill of Human Rights,[3] (2) are seldom clearly covered in the news.

The data distribution over 31 days is laid out in Figure 4.1. The data show the sum mentions of the international human rights principles in combination with the sum mentions of the humanitarian laws and *jus cogens* over this period. It is clear that there is a fluctuation over this month and a variation of counts throughout this period. These counts were obtained from those news packages that had at least one mention of the international human rights laws and principles. It is, therefore, obvious why the line connecting the dots never falls to zero. Since the focus of the research was on human rights, the irrelevant news packages during this month were purposefully left out. The peak of the distribution in Figure 4.1 is on July 22, 2014. On this

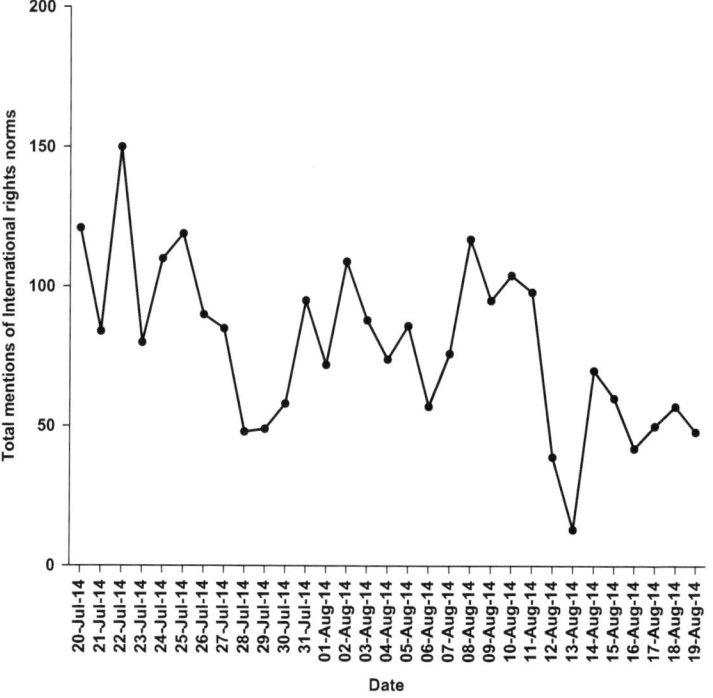

Figure 4.1 The distribution of total mentions of international rights norms over 31 days.

day at the primetime news hour, 14 news packages contained some mention of international human rights principles, humanitarian laws, or *jus cogens*. The trough of this distribution falls on August 13, 2014, which only included three news packages containing any mention of international human rights principles, humanitarian laws, or *jus cogens*.

While the results are significant enough so far, they become even more telling when the data are further broken down. What stands out from the analysis of the data is the different weight that is put on foreign versus domestic news coverage of events, which bear any mention of human rights and humanitarian principles. The top line in Figure 4.2 shows the number of news packages that focus on foreign events and the bottom line shows the number of news packages that focus on domestic events, all containing some human rights language. The figure shows that a significant number of news packages that have any mention of human rights and humanitarian principles are allocated to foreign news.

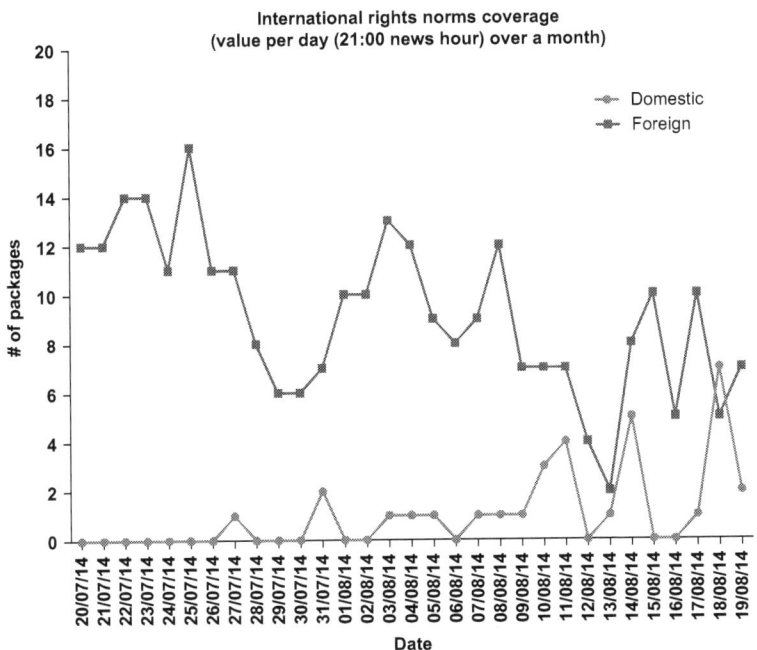

Figure 4.2 Foreign versus domestic news coverage containing international human rights and humanitarian principles during the month under study.

The Significance of Human Rights Coverage

An unpaired *t*-test was carried out to reconfirm the true significance of the distinction between domestic and foreign news coverage. The unpaired *t*-test allowed for the comparison of the difference between the means of both groups with the standard error of the difference. In other words, the mean values of domestic and foreign news coverage in these packages were calculated per day over a month. These values are bar graphed in Figure 4.3. There is a considerable gap between the two bars, with the gray bar representing the foreign news coverage and the black bar representing the domestic news coverage. The results of the *t*-test show that the two-tailed *P* value is less than 0.0001, which means that the two variables are significantly different. The *P* value summary is ****, and the differences among means are statistically significant (significance cut-off $P < 0.05$).

Not only is it important to know which events—domestic or foreign—with the highest use of human rights language get covered, it is also important to note where they are specifically situated in

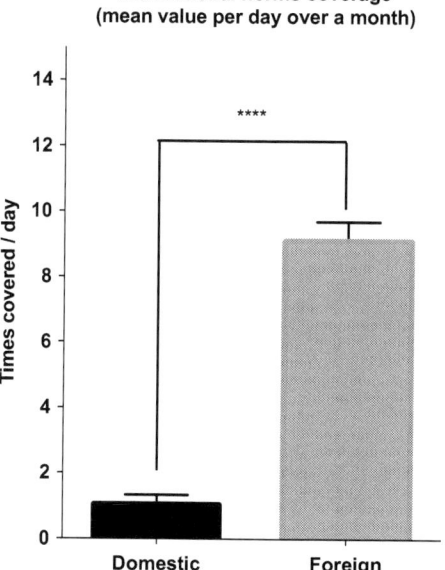

International norms coverage
(mean value per day over a month)

Figure 4.3 Mentions of human rights terms in foreign versus domestic news coverage (mean value per day over a month)—data in graphs reflect mean ± standard error of mean (SEM). The summary $P < 0.0001$ using unpaired *t*-test.

the news program. The one-hour news program was, therefore, divided into five categories or news package placements: (1) 00:00–2:29; (2) 2:30–14:59; (3) 15:00–29:59; (4) 30:00–44:59; (5) 45:00–End of program. The average sum of the news packages in each of these categories was then turned into a bar graph in Figure 4.4. The five bar graphs were then compared using an ordinary one-way analysis of variance (ANOVA). As is clearly shown in Figure 4.4, the bar with the highest number of packages containing any use of human rights language falls between 15 and 30 minutes of the news programs. That is if we count in the first three-minute news package placement, which is an introductory package and features the list of lead or main news stories. If we exclude the introductory package and just focus on the actual news packages, then the tallest bar in Figure 4.4 falls in the "lead position," which, according to Iyengar and Kinder, is "substantially more influential" (3) than if it was placed in the middle or the end position.

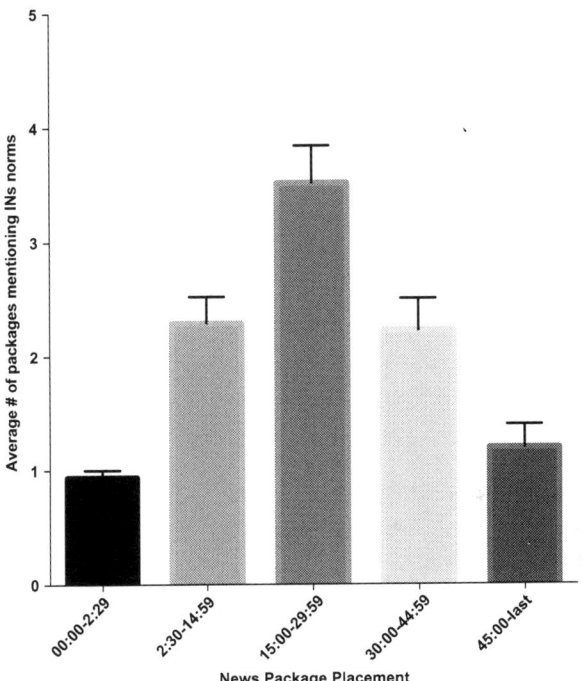

Figure 4.4 News placement of the average number of packages with mentions of international rights norms (humanitarian and human rights)—data in graphs reflect mean ± SEM. The summary *P* < 0.0001 using one-way ANOVA.

The ANOVA test results are also significant. The P value for the whole test was less than 0.0001, which means that the variables are significantly different. The P value summary is ****, and the differences among means are statistically significant ($P < 0.05$).

It is also important to know how long the packages containing any international human rights terms or categories took to be presented. The results show that the length of 40% of the news packages was between 1:00 and 2:59 minutes. Twenty-six percent of them were presented within 3:00 to 4:59 minutes and 21% took 5:00 to 9:59 minutes to be broadcast. The data were also categorized based on themes since certain events, especially for foreign news packages, tended to repeat themselves.

Conclusion

Among all the subjects covered, two themes of foreign news events stood out. These themes were in relation to Gaza-Israel armed conflict and the death of Michael Brown in Ferguson, United States. Therefore, one package containing the highest mention of international human rights and humanitarian norms related to each of these themes was selected for a multimodal critical discourse analysis (MCDA), which will be discussed in Chapter 5.

Choosing two domestic news packages that had a high usage of human rights language proved more difficult since there were not that many to choose from. During the analysis, two news packages stood out. A news package on the Judiciary's press conference was chosen for MCDA not because it had the highest count of human rights terms but because Gholam-Hossein Mohseni-Eje'i, Iran's Prosecutor General and spokesperson for the Judiciary, mentioned the execution of three individuals in Iran. Such direct language regarding human rights violations was rarely found in domestic news. The second news package on Iran's Supreme Leader's clemency or commutation of punishments was selected for analysis, once again not because it had the highest count of human rights terms but because Khamenei, who is the current Supreme Leader of Iran and who has the highest authority in the country, "pardons" or "reduces" the sentences of a group of convicts on the occasion of "Eid-e Fetr"[4] (4). This news item has a clear implicit human rights implication, which may expose certain hegemonic power and underlying ideologies. It may also reveal certain power relations, which would contribute to a fundamental liberating force (5). The results of the domestic news analysis will be discussed in Chapter 6.

Notes

1 Paragraph 13, 2011 (CCPR/C/SR.2834).
2 These terms were counted only in relation to civilians and not combatants.
3 International Bill of Human Rights consists of the UN General Assembly Resolution 217 A (III) and two international treaties called the Universal Declaration of Human Rights and the International Covenant on Civil and Political Rights (ICCPR). The ICCPR consists of two Optional Protocols and the International Covenant on Economic, Social and Cultural Rights.
4 "The holiday at the end of Ramadan that marks the finish of a month of daylight fasting."

References

1. OHCHR. *International Human Rights Law.* OHCHR: The Office of the High Commissioner for Human Rights; 2019. Available from: https://www.ohchr.org/en/professionalinterest/Pages/InternationalLaw.aspx.
2. AHRC. *Fact sheet 5: The International Bill of Rights.* Australian Human Rights Commission; 2009. Available from: https://www.humanrights.gov.au/sites/default/files/content/education/hr_explained/download/FS5_International.pdf.
3. Iyengar S, Kinder DR. *News that matters: Television and American opinion (updated edition).* Updated ed. Chicago, IL: University of Chicago Press; Bristol: University Presses Marketing [distributor]; 2010:43.
4. Kurzman C. *The unthinkable revolution in Iran.* Cambridge, MA: Harvard University Press; 2004:62.
5. Machin D, Mayr A. *How to do critical discourse analysis: A multimodal introduction.* London: SAGE; 2012:15.

5 MCDA of Foreign Events in IRIB News

Introduction

The sharp difference between how human rights and humanitarian principles are used to report on foreign versus domestic events was quantitatively illustrated in Chapter 4. In this chapter, two foreign news packages will be qualitatively analyzed using multimodal critical discourse analysis (MCDA) to determine how human rights and humanitarian laws are used in the Islamic Republic of Iran Broadcasting's (IRIB) news programs. The first is regarding the case of Michael Brown's shooting in the United States, which is regarding an African American teen who was shot by a white police officer in Ferguson, Missouri. Protests ensued in the aftermath. In addition to the United States, IRIB's news also targets Israel. The Israel-Gaza conflict is of particular interest and often repeated on IRIB—at least this was the case in August 2014, when this research was carried out. It is safe to assume that it will be as long as the conflict goes on. One news package on this issue is multimodally analyzed second to see how this story, which is heavily imbued with human rights terms, is portrayed.

The Case of Michael Brown's Shooting in Ferguson, Missouri

The news package on the case of Michael Brown's shooting in Ferguson was one of the most repeated packages with the highest use of human rights language in August 2014 when this research was carried out. MCDA was applied to this foreign news package with the aim of unraveling any hidden ideologies expressed in the IRIB's news deliverance, thus revealing constructed power relations between the agents represented in the news.

Lexical Analysis of IRIB's Coverage of the Brown Case

The news segment begins by showing a male anchor named Reza Hosseinzadeh reading the news heading: "The expansion of the scope of protests against discrimination in different cities of America." The heading contains two words that relate to two very explicit principles of international human rights law: protests and discrimination. Indeed, lexical analysis of the whole text demonstrates the predominant use of the words "protests" (*e'terazat*), "demonstrations" (*tazahorat*), "racist" (*nejadparast*), and "discrimination" (*tab'iz*). These are explicit human rights terms, illustrating that the author of the text or the producer of the news had a fair knowledge of these principles. IRIB producers' knowledge about the principles of international human rights and humanitarian laws becomes more evident when an interviewee is shown saying, "It is very sad to see the police violating the fundamental rights of my fellow citizens."

Even though Hosseinzadeh is only shown briefly at the beginning of the footage, his demeanor denotes IRIB's intentions. His eyebrows and voice are raised on the words "expansion" and "different cities of America" when reading the news heading. Hosseinzadeh then reads his second line: "Barack Obama's request for stifling people's anger failed, and the protests against the violence and discriminatory behaviors of the American police spread to numerous cities." In this sentence, his emphasis is on "stifle," "failed," and "numerous cities." In his next sentence, "[T]housands of people in the cities of Ferguson of Missouri, New York, and Los Angeles demonstrated in reaction to the death of Michael Brown, a black youth from Ferguson," his voice and eyebrows are raised on the words "thousands of people."

These accentuations on specific words are especially important when they are combined with the pronouns "they" and "we" in the next sentence as when a young black woman says, "they are killing off young black men every day; it is almost like our lives do not have any worth." This tactic aligns the viewer alongside black people as victims and against the police as villains.

The impression that the package is giving is that the United States is a divided country. On one side, there are the "people" and on the opposite side are the "police," and even Obama cannot reconcile that. Despite his request, the public demonstrations against the police expand and Obama comes across as a powerless person whose attempts to "stifle" the anger and stop the spread of "thousands of people" to "numerous cities" "fail." In addition, Obama's functional title, the "President," is withheld in this news package, diminishing the importance of his social role and weakening his authority. There is also aggregation used in the opening lines. Both the participants (thousands of people) and cities (numerous) are quantified and treated as statistics. This manner of quantification implies that research has been done objectively and that the statistics are credible (1).

IRIB's attempt to highlight antagonism in the United States does not end here. In one instance, the neutral structuring verb "say" is used. The anchor is heard saying, "protestors say the face of the police has changed from a force protecting the public to an oppressive force." The use of the verb "say" represents the protestors as neutral and innocent of any wrongdoing. Therefore, violation, racism, and discrimination are solely attributed to the police as a government apparatus. IRIB seems to take this one-sided approach to report on the violations of the international human rights law by the United States, and it is an excuse for it to belittle the US government that has unleashed the police on its people but has a hard time managing it.

The overlexicalization of words such as "youth" in relation to black people who are targeted by the police is used to create further antagonism. This overlexicalization, even though a fact in the case of Michael Brown, has been generalized for all black youth. The excessive use of the term creates sympathy for the youth since the word "youth" is synonymous with "innocence" and "vulnerability" (1). The black youth are also portrayed as weak agents who need to be "supported" and their rights "vindicated" by their white compatriots. A young white woman protester is shown saying, "I hope these incidents are the beginning of a fundamental change. It is very important for us to support the black community in America and show them that we are by their side and seek justice."

Further lexical analysis of this news package reveals that facts have been replaced by abstractions and generalizations. These are signs of ideologies at work. In one instance, for example, the anchor states, "protests against the violence and discriminatory behaviors of the American police spread to numerous cities." We are not told what these discriminatory behaviors are and what kind of violence has been directed toward the protestors. In another instance, we are told, "In the sixth day of the protests against the racist behaviors in the United States, people and different political and social groups are now protesting against the reaction of the police towards protestors." Once again, we are not told what and who these "political and social groups" are.

In general, what is missing in this news package are the actual relevant facts of the incident. Who was Michael Brown? How old was he?

What were the circumstances surrounding his death? Were there any witnesses? Were the individuals who testified, his friends or bystanders? Who was the police officer that killed Michael Brown? Was he on trial? Was he convicted? There are no opposing views presented in the news package, and there are no statements from the chief of police or the lawyer of the accused police officer. These details have been suppressed for the ideological reason of drawing attention to and emphasizing the racist behavior of the police toward the black people and their violent behavior toward protestors, two fundamental human rights issues in the United States.

Three of the interviewees shown in this news package are a young black woman, a young black man, and a young white woman. These individuals have only been represented by their function[1] as protestors and not by their nomination.[2] In addition, throughout the text, words such as "demonstrators" and "protestors" are used as functionalization to moderately dehumanize the people and accentuate only the roles they are playing while giving them some legitimacy (1).

In contrast, three other interviewees have all been both functionalized and nominated, hence more authoritative: Charles Barron introduced as "the former Party leader of the black people in New York," a *Washington Post* journalist and researcher by the name of Radley Balko, and a retired US Army Lieutenant General by the name of Russel Honore. Not only do they sound more official, but they also sound more personal through functionalization and nomination, respectively. The news package also includes an unnamed US Marine Corps.

IRIB's Voiceover

Part of the news package includes an interview with *Washington Post* correspondent, Radley Balko, who appeared on the cable news station, CNN. In the interview, Balko was asked what he saw when he looked at a few photos of military-grade weapons in the streets of Ferguson. His reply was,

> I saw the continuation of a trend that's been going on for about 35 years. The policing in America has been becoming increasingly militarized. We've seen literally millions of pieces of military equipment, equipment that was designed for use on a battlefield—you know, we're talking tanks, armed personnel careers, helicopters, grenade launchers, M-16s—transferred to police departments across the country (2).

In IRIB's voiceover translation, the beginning of Balko's sentence has been changed to *"this situation* is the continuation of a trend..." instead. This change is subtle, but it is of importance when the context changes. In the IRIB version, this sentence comes right after the one by another interviewee, a veteran US marine, who says "responding with tanks and snipers to a peaceful protest is ridiculous." This combination gives the impression that peaceful protests have been continuously cracked down by tanks and snipers for 35 years rather than the militarization of the police gradually taking place over 35 years. The crackdown of peaceful protest is a violation of Article 20(1) of the Universal Declaration of Human Rights where it is clearly stated "[e]veryone has the right to freedom of peaceful assembly and association" (3).

Furthermore, by quoting Balko's specific use of battlefield equipment terminologies such as "tanks, armed personnel careers, helicopters, grenade launchers, M-16s," which connote specialist knowledge, the news package becomes more authoritative (1). Balko also says this equipment was "transferred to police departments across the country." This statement is an abstraction since we are not told who has done the transferring and why.

Following Balko, the second functionalized and nominated interviewee, retired US Lieutenant General Russel Honore, is shown saying, "the responsibility of [the] police is to protect people. The fact that the police officers appear in public with military and war equipment aimed at people conveys a very bad message." The actual footage that IRIB uses for this voiceover translation is from the CNN interview where Honore says,

> We're there to protect people. In that case, we were there to evacuate them and provide them [with] food and water. There's no need to point a weapon at civilians. And officers do that; they need to go through retraining. You should not point combat-type weapons directly at people (2).

The original transcript reveals that Honore's response was concerning the comment of CNN anchor who stated,

> I remember that one moment in New Orleans where one of the officers pointed his gun at someone, and you took him to task for it. And it seems that's what the captain here is doing, very similarly [*sic*] to what you did in New Orleans (2).

The comparison reveals that, first of all, the information is misrepresented. One case is taken and generalized. Second, at least in this case, the police officer that overstepped his boundaries did get reprimanded for it. This information is suppressed in the IRIB news package.

What IRIB may have intended to use, as its footage, is Honore's next response:

> The people have to always remember that you are there to protect them. And you will only go after people who put them in danger. And it's not the job of the police or any service of the armed forces to threaten people with weapons. You're there to protect people and to be prepared to deal with people who may break the law. But you're there to protect the people. And they need to sense that from you. But when you have an officer, as we saw in the last 24 hours, setting [sic] there, looking through a scope into a crowd, that sends the wrong message (2).

There are still discrepancies in the voiceover translation even if the earlier statement was intended to be used by IRIB producers. The voiceover translation seems to have blown the response out of proportion. "An officer" is changed to "police officers" and "a scope" is changed to "military and war equipment."

Another interviewee by the name of Charles Barron is shown saying,

> If the issue of police brutality does not get addressed, the reactions and insurgencies similar to Ferguson will be repeated. All the racist police officers must be eliminated from the system because we are determined to fight for justice and our rights.

Barron's exact sentence in the footage, as can be heard behind the voiceover translation, is

> so we are saying to this nation, to this city, to this state that all oppressive laws must go, all sick racist police must go because we are going to fight for our justice. We are going to do whatever is necessary to protect ourselves.

By using deontic modality through the word "must," Barron is expressing urgency. The use of this deontic modality is expected of him because of his political activities. Through its use, he is also appealing to a certain power that is not mentioned (1).

Except for this sentence, where only those police who are racist are targeted, there are 11 other times where the police are represented as a generic type. This generalization gives the impression that all police officers in the United States are racist and violent (1). The name of the police officer who killed Michael Brown is not mentioned at all. This suppression prevents the viewers from becoming intimate with any police as an individual and getting acquainted with his or her side of the story.

Transitivity Analysis

A transitivity analysis indicates that both the people and the US police are represented as agents of action but in different ways. In this news package, we are only told about the action of the police who do the violating, killing, shooting, murdering, and oppressing. These are representations of material processes[3] that have consequences but have been conveyed by the protestors. The people of America are agents of action as well through demonstrating, protesting, supporting, and fighting for justice and rights, which are also material processes. Interestingly, the people are simultaneously passive agents or the target of the police at whom the actions are directed (1). The people are "responded to," "murdered," "killed," "shot at," "confronted," "oppressed," and "discriminated against." Because people of America are represented as both active and passive agents in this news package, it is not surprising to see more than one verb process at work.

In the case of the people, there are mental processes that allow the viewer to get close to their feelings and thought processes (1). The reactions of the people are characterized to be that of "anger" and "sadness," which encourage the viewer to feel both outrage and empathy. Activating the people on positive actions and passivating them on negative actions contribute to depictions of power (1). As yet another participant, since Obama's material action fails to have any outcome, his agency is foregrounded representing him as a weak agent. Moreover, the actions of the police have not been accentuated as much as those of the people. It is the people who have "expanded" their forces to other cities. Therefore, they are the most powerful out of all three participants.

The use of the prepositional phrase "for" in the sentence "Barack Obama's request for stifling people's anger failed" provides context for the dominant clause, "Barack Obama's request failed." This prepositional phrase also diminishes the responsibility of the actions of the "angry" people (1). Later in the news, an interviewee is shown saying, "all the racist police officers must be eliminated from the system because we are determined to fight for justice and our rights." The conjunction "because" separates the dominant clause, "all the racist police officers must be eliminated from the system," from the subordinate clause, "because we are determined to fight for justice and our rights." Since the subordinate clause is positioned after the dominant clause, more emphasis is put on the racist police than the fight for justice and rights. This analysis strengthens the possible ideology behind this news package. IRIB producers seem to be making an effort to demonstrate the presence of racist police in the United States rather than the global need for equal rights and justice.

IRIB News and Visual Representation

The visual analysis of the Michael Brown news package also provides evidence of the underlying message intended for IRIB's audience. To begin with, some footage used in the news, for example, the footage of a US Marine Corps interviewee, was extracted without reference. In the case of the US Marine Corps, the footage was obtained from the archives of the Associated Press (AP), which was broadcast the day before, on August 14, 2014 (4). Extracting certain information out of context and inserting it where it best suits may have a purpose. This manipulation may suggest some ideology at work where only certain sentences uttered by individuals are used to achieve an end and convey a specific message. In this case, the message is somewhat clear that the US police are racist and they discriminately kill and violate the human rights of their people, more specifically black youth. Individuals with various degrees of authority are included in the news package to support this message.

The "Authoritative" Interviewees

The unnamed US Marine turns out to be Corporal Tyson Manker, a veteran who served during the 2003 invasion of Iraq (5). By comparing Figure 5.1 (top image), which is an image taken from the original footage produced by the AP, with the bottom image in Figure 5.1, taken from footage used by IRIB, it is clear that the AP logo from the top right-hand corner has been cropped out and the "Channel 1 News" logo has been placed in the lower right-hand corner instead. Perhaps, this manipulation was done to avoid copyright

Figure 5.1 The image of US Marine Corps from the original footage of the Associated Press (top) and the image of US Marine Corps from Associated Press footage used by IRIB (bottom).

issues. The footage shown by IRIB is blurry and of low resolution compared to the original, which may suggest that the footage was not directly downloaded from the AP site but was rather filmed as it was being broadcast. The creation of such low modality could also have been intentionally created if we are to assume that the IRIB editors are impeccable at their job. The images of soldiers, politicians, and criminals in media are frequently found to be in "completely decontextualized, low naturalistic settings" because the intention is to "symbolize" their "feelings and reactions" and not to document what they are doing (1).

What is also interesting is the editing done on the footage of Radley Balko by IRIB. Balko can be heard in the background saying, "dressed like a soldier and trained like a soldier" before the voiceover translation takes over. Halfway through the voiceover translation, there is a very abrupt cut, and Balko is again heard saying, "dressed like a soldier and trained like a soldier" in the background. This deliberate editing choice suggests that there was not enough footage of Balko for the duration of the voiceover translation. The original CNN interview is relatively long, but it includes others besides Balko. Soon after Balko starts speaking, the frame changes to show Balko and Honore together with the anchor (Figure 5.2). To avoid revealing that these two interviews were part of one news package, IRIB editors had to use the same footage of Balko twice.

CNN interviewed Balko and Honore on police militarization and the situation in Ferguson together. However, taken out of context in the IRIB news coverage, it seems that Balko and Honore are speaking individually on different occasions, which adds to the breadth of this issue and the underlying opinion being portrayed by IRIB. The original interview aired on *CNN Tonight* on August 14, 2014 (6). The CNN logo (Figures 5.3 and 5.4, top images) has been completely covered by the "iribnews.ir" logo (Figures 5.3 and 5.4, bottom images).

Figure 5.2 The original CNN footage showing Balko and Honore together with the anchor.

Figure 5.3 The image of Radley Balko from the original footage of the CNN
(top) and the image of Radley Balko from CNN footage used by
IRIB (bottom).

The positioning of every single person shown in this news package
is also curious. All the interviewees and the anchor are shown in close
shots positioned at the same height as the viewer. This positioning
allows the viewer to get personal with the interviewees or participants and to become intimate with their inner states and feelings as
ordinary people. Furthermore, some of the participants, including
the anchor, are found looking right at the viewer. Their gaze along
with their proximity to the camera portrays them as open and sincere.

Figure 5.4 The image of Russel Honore from the original footage of the CNN (top) and the image of Russel Honore from CNN footage used by IRIB (bottom).

The gazes of some other interviewees are slightly off-frame. Their close shots along with the off-frame gazes allow the viewer to observe these interviewees objectively and take their thoughts into consideration (1). Out of all, Charles Barron, another authoritative interviewee, is shown in a side-on close-up (Figure 5.5). This positioning shows his togetherness. Even though the viewers only observe and are not directly involved in his thoughts, they are prompted to consider his concerns (1).

Figure 5.5 Charles Barron, an interviewee, shown in a side-on close-up.

The IRIB Anchor

Since all the footage shown of the protests are from foreign news agencies, the only original IRIB footage is that of the anchor speaking from the studio. The male anchor is wearing a simple dark gray shirt and light gray jacket. The color gray connotes conservativeness, which is expected considering the many memos from the Iranian authorities to government agencies regarding appearance and attire. An official directive from former Iranian Prime Minister[4] (7) in the 1980s instructed female employees to wear "loose and long manteaus and pants with a simple design and thick and unicolor fabric.... The selected manteaus and pants must be chosen from dignified colors. Dark-blue, brown, gray and black are preferable." Male employees are to wear "simple, ordinary, long sleeve and loose clothing in a way that does not mimic the Western culture and which is befitting of male employees" (8). In the Michael Brown news package, the male anchor has a serious and expressionless face. The only features that stand out are the movement of his eyebrows and the tone of his voice (Figure 5.6).

The Israel-Gaza Conflict

This news segment on the conflict between Israel and Gaza starts at minute 5:56 and ends at minute 15:01 out of the total program time of 52:26 minutes, positioning the story in the lead and thus increasing its

Figure 5.6 IRIB anchor named Reza Hosseinzadeh.

influential. The conflict is covered three times during the news hour, but the news package analyzed here is an exclusive report on the conflict covered by a male reporter who is not identified. The IRIB anchor is once again Reza Hosseinzadeh.

Violations of the International Humanitarian and Customary Laws

The package opens with 23 seconds of night shelling and bombing footage. Then, an ambulance is shown in the morning rushing to the hospital, and paramedics are shown carrying small children as they run from the ambulances into the hospital. The next scene shows corpses of people lying in the streets over which the unknown reporter starts reading his opening lines with heart-rending music in the background. He states,

> Mass killing, war crime, ethnic cleansing, another Sabra and Shatila (9),[5] the second Deir Yassin (10),[6] genocide, these are the names that media groups and witnesses attribute to the new series of crimes committed by Zionists in Shuja'iyya of Gaza Strip. But, the images transmitted through camera frames are indescribable.

In this news package, there is an overrepresentation of the words "children" and "women"—they are mentioned nine times. Women and children are thought to be the most vulnerable and innocent in society, and they are portrayed as having no part in the activities of the organized resistance group, Hamas. These women and children are, therefore, civilians. Based on rule five of the norms of customary international humanitarian law, "civilians are persons who are not members of the armed forces" (11) and should "enjoy protection… unless and for such time as they take a direct part in hostilities" (12).[7]

In the report, the Gaza Health Ministry spokesperson specifically details who has died. His voiceover translation states, "The Zionist regime has targeted residential homes in Shuja'iyya since dawn this morning, and, after bombing residential homes, it turned its attention to the killing of women, children, elderly men, and civilians in this area." Women, children, and the elderly are civilians. However, the fact that they are specifically mentioned as opposed to just the word "civilian" communicates a stronger sense of outrage since women, children, and the elderly are thought to be defenseless and innocent. The specific and repeated mention of women and children as victims of the conflict also legitimizes the activities and actions of the resistance group. This portrayal demonizes Israel and draws on the sympathy and conscience of the world community to take action against it. Though vulnerable and innocent, however, the children are not shown as weak characters. A middle-aged male interviewee is shown saying "all our little children and daughters want to get in line with the resistance fighters."

The spokesperson's statement mentioned earlier also points to the fact that no distinction was made between civilian objects and military objectives, which is a violation of a norm of customary international law. Rule seven of the international humanitarian law states "the parties to the conflict must at all times distinguish between civilian objects and military objectives. Attacks may only be directed against military objectives. Attacks must not be directed against civilian objects" (11). Rule nine also specifically states that "civilian objects are all objects that are not military objectives." Therefore, "civilian areas," "towns," "cities," "residential areas," "hospitals," "schools," and "places of worship" are considered *prima facie* civilian objects that, according to rule 10, must be "protected against attack, unless and for such time as they are military objectives" (11).

Another word that is repeatedly mentioned in the news package is the word "martyr," which is used to describe the men, women, and children who were killed in Gaza. On the other hand, the word "killed" and not "martyred" is used for the Israeli soldiers who lost their lives in conflict. By attributing "martyrdom" to Palestinians only, far greater importance is placed on their lives, and a definitive distinction is made between Israelis and Palestinians, which encourages, at least, the Muslim viewers to form religious discrimination against the Jews.

Non-civilian Israelis are not mentioned at all even though in one instance we are told: "in response to Israeli attacks, the resistance combatants launched hundreds of missiles on Tel Aviv and other cities in the Occupied Territories." The actions of Hamas are again endorsed since they are always in "response to" the attacks of Israel—they never seem to be the initiators. Even though it is reported that "hundreds of missiles" were launched toward "Tel Aviv and other cities" in Israel, some questions remain unanswered. For example, how many civilians were killed in Israel following these attacks? Were any residential properties damaged in Israel? How many Israeli civilians were injured? How many of these included women and children? By only mentioning the death of Israeli soldiers, it appears that Hamas has not violated any humanitarian law and has only targeted the Israeli military.

The lexical choices used to describe the conflict concerning Gaza are subjective and sacred (1). "Residential homes," "mosques," and "hospitals," instead of just buildings, have a more intimate and familiar sense to them. "Homes" signify safety and stability; "mosques" signify sacredness and faith; and "hospitals" signify hope and healing. Using specific building types in the program communicates that the people of Gaza are in need of special protection. Such an approach is designed to produce a strong emotional response from the viewer (1).

Other parts of this news package allude to further international humanitarian laws. In one instance, the reporter states, "Bodies of tens of women, men, old, and young lie in every corner of rubble-stricken streets of Shuja'iyya in the east of Gaza." "Zionists' heavy air raids, artillery, and tank attack, which started since dawn, did not allow for even the collection of a multitude of bodies." Rule 112 of the international humanitarian law states that "whenever circumstances permit, and particularly after an engagement, each party to the conflict must, without delay, take all possible measures to reach for, collect and evacuate the dead without adverse distinction" (11). This rule could be interpreted in different ways if it were to be taken out of context. "Particularly after an engagement" gives the impression that after every engagement a temporary ceasefire must take effect to allow for the collection of the dead. "Whenever circumstances permit" and "take all possible measures," however, turn this rule into "an obligation of means rather than results" (13). The wording has taken into account possible difficulties of immediate collection such as the "ongoing military operations" (13). Whatever the case may be, IRIB's presentation comes across as emphasizing Israel's violation of this humanitarian law.

"Journalists" and "medical personnel" were also reported to be among the dead. It is not clear whether these journalists were independent journalists or war correspondents. However, since the news package emphasizes the death of civilians, the viewer is encouraged to assume that the journalists were independent and hence civilians, in which case rule 34 of the international humanitarian law has been violated. This rule holds that "civilian journalists engaged in professional missions in areas of armed conflict must be respected and protected as long as they are not taking a direct part in hostilities" (11). In addition, rule 25 states that "medical personnel exclusively assigned to medical duties must be respected and protected in all circumstances. They lose their protection if they commit, outside their humanitarian function, acts harmful to the enemy" (11).

Attacking medical transports is also a violation of the international humanitarian norms. The Gaza Health Ministry's spokesperson is, once again, shown saying, "to complete its crimes, the Zionist regime targeted the ambulances as well. As a result, five ambulances were hit." Rule 29 of the international humanitarian law states that "medical transports assigned exclusively to medical transportation must be respected and protected in all circumstances. They lose their protection if they are being used, outside their humanitarian function, to commit acts harmful to the enemy" (11).

The protections inherent in the customary and humanitarian laws are dependent on the neutrality of civilians, journalists, and aid workers. This news package gives no indication that civilians may have played a role in the conflict. However, we are invited into the thoughts of two civilians who come across as strong characters willing to give all they have for the conflict. One is a mother who has lost two of her children in the conflict. She states,

> I thank God because of these martyrs. I have given up two martyrs and am ready to give more. What are important are God and His pleasure. I thank God that our faith is strong. God bless my children. Goodbye till heaven.

Visually, in a close-up shot, she looks right at the camera and engages with the viewer (Figure 5.7). Consequently, the viewer can get close to

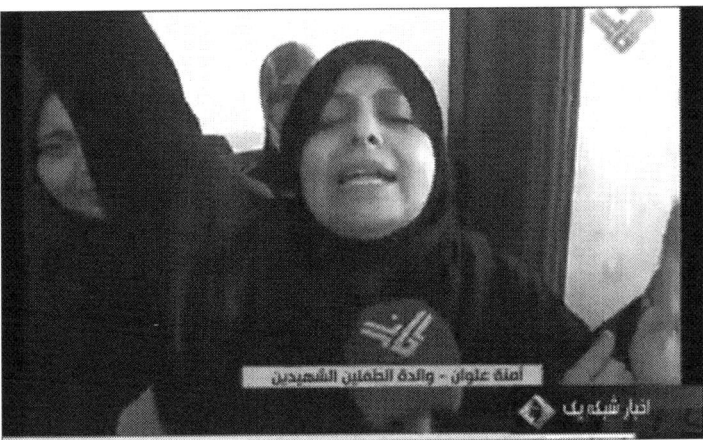

Figure 5.7 A female civilian interviewee in Israel-Gaza conflict.

this civilian and get acquainted with her private thoughts and feelings. These two combined semiotic choices portray this woman as open and sincere.

The second civilian interviewed is a middle-aged man who states,

> In order to create fear and terror among us and for us to declare our hatred towards the resistance, the occupier regime targets us. But, we are all ready to get in line with the resistance. All our little children and daughters want to get in line with the resistance fighters. We are all in line with the resistance from this very moment and say that we must either die or live freely.

While this does not sound like a neutral citizen, he blames the world community for not protecting the innocent Muslims. He states,

> The world is cruel. The whole world is cruel. If there were any conscientious people in the world, they would have protected us because they know that we are innocent. It is for this reason that I say the whole world, from Arab countries and our leaders to others, are all cruel and conspire against us because if they were Muslims and even knew anything about Islam, they would see that a large number get martyred here every day. They would, as a result, take action but they are not taking any action. If Israeli soldiers were getting killed, then they would have taken some action.

In this news story, there is an overlexicalization of the word "Muslim," which is repetitive and overemphasized. This "over-persuasion" is a cue to ideological dominance—only "true" Muslims understand empathy and take action to protect the innocent (1). There are also obvious generalizations and abstractions. We are not told who "the world" is and who the "others" are. This vagueness conceals power relations. We are also not told what type of action is expected by whom or what kind of action would be required if the victims were Israeli soldiers.

This citizen is also shown in close-up, but he is not looking directly at the camera (Figure 5.8). Instead, there is a side view of his face, which makes him somewhat detached from the viewer, giving him an air of togetherness, despite the chaos that one would expect in a conflict. This arrangement also connotes that his position is shared with the viewers, and they are persuaded to affiliate with his worries and beliefs (1).

Since a partial focus of the news package is about the suffering of Palestinians as civilians, it is not surprising to find these images in close shots. The Israeli soldiers, on the other hand, are shown in medium and long shots (Figure 5.9). The difference lies in the fact that the audience is not meant to become intimate with the Israeli soldiers and to consider their thoughts and concerns at a personal level.

Figure 5.8 A male civilian interviewee in the Israel-Gaza conflict.

Figure 5.9 Israeli soldiers shown in a long shot.

Ideological Squaring: Us versus Them

In this news package, there are two main sides—Israel and Palestine. We are not explicitly told which one is bad and which one is good. However, the structural oppositions or "ideological squaring" (14) encourages the participants to be evaluated in specific ways. Ideological squaring involves four moves:

1   Express/emphasize information that is positive about Us.
2   Express/emphasize information that is negative about Them.
3   Suppress/de-emphasize information that is positive about Them.
4   Suppress/de-emphasize information that is negative about Us.

In relation to Israel or "them," word choices such as "Zionist enemy," "occupier regime," "savage crime," "horrible crime," "war crime," "genocide," "mass murder," "ethnic cleansing," "anger," and "fear" are used. In the case of Palestine or "us," words such as "innocent," "lament," "martyr," "strong faith," "heaven," "resistance," "conscientious," "noble death," and "defense and offense power" are used. Based on ideological squaring, these expressions and suppressions contribute to the overall tactic of "positive self-presentation" or "face-keeping" and "negative other-presentation" (14).

The lexical terms "mass murder," "genocide," "war crime," and "ethnic cleansing" in relation to Israel are also crimes broadly covered under the international humanitarian law and are described as "crimes against humanity." Based on rule 156 of the customary international humanitarian law, "serious violation of international law constitute war crimes" (11).

Showing real grieving Palestinians create individualization. Viewers are encouraged to feel empathy for the Palestinians and to feel closer to them. However, the death of Israeli soldiers is announced as a triumph. The reporter says, "In response to Israeli attacks, the resistance combatants launched hundreds of missiles on Tel Aviv and other cities in the Occupied Territories." "Last night, a column of Zionist infantries in Al-Tuffah, East of Gaza, fell into the ambush of resistance forces where 33 of the Zionist military got killed, and their weapons were either destroyed or confiscated." In this sentence, the "Zionist military" is generic. Nowhere in the package do viewers interact with individual Israelis. Giving a sense of pride for their "response" to Israeli attacks, the reporter says, "Up until now, the resistance forces have destroyed seven tanks and personnel carriers, which belonged to the Zionists." Israeli soldiers are also represented as a type. However, since Iran does not recognize Israel as a state, it refers to Israel as a Zionist regime. Those living in the "occupied" territory, including the Israeli civilians, are also considered Zionists. Therefore, by placing this generic category in the news, the news story is given a "racialized slant."

Hamas, on the other hand, is functionalized as the "resistance combatants." In this case, functionalization sounds more official than what is attributed to Israel and thus connotes legitimacy. In one instance of the segment, the Israeli government is functionalized but also referred to as the "occupant regime," making this functionalization negative. The objectivation of the Israeli government to the "occupant regime" and the "Zionist enemy" throughout the package reduces its humanity. Objectivation is commonly done in ideological squaring. By objectifying Israel, the moral issues surrounding the conflict between Israel and Palestine come across as reasonable on the part of Hamas, also referred to as the "resistance combatants" and horrific on the part of Israel.

The Blame Game

Besides the violations of the international laws, both sides renounce responsibility for the conflict by playing the blame game. In one instance, the IRIB reporter states,

> Palestine's resistance groups have emphasized that they have not accepted the ceasefire that Israel has in mind because it will

neither end the siege of Gaza, nor will it prevent the recurrence of attacks or provide the possibility of medicines and foodstuffs to reach the people of Gaza.

This sentence suggests that Israel does not allow food and medicine to reach the civilians. Rule 55 of the customary international humanitarian law states "The parties to the conflict must allow and facilitate rapid and unimpeded passage of humanitarian relief for civilians in need, which is impartial in character and conducted without any adverse distinction, subject to their right of control" (11).

At one point in the news, the reporter says,

the Zionist regime and the USA claim to support the ceasefire while today Israel was not prepared to accept the request made by the Red Cross for a three-hour ceasefire and the extraction of bodies and the wounded from Shuja'iyya.

By contrast, the next sentence underscores Hamas's cooperation with the Red Cross when Hamas's spokesperson states, "The Red Cross contacted Hamas today and introduced a proposal for a few-hour ceasefire so that it could extract the wounded and the martyrs. We accepted this proposal, but the occupiers opposed it."

It is very clear from the language used in the program thus far that IRIB's producers are familiar with the international humanitarian laws and the Red Cross's mission as a provider for war victims and a promoter of international humanitarian law (15). The news package has been put together with enough knowledge of international human rights principles to not only point out Israel's violations of it but also to appeal to the emotions of viewers and incite hatred against the "Zionist regime" and encourage sympathy toward the "resistance group."

Visual Analysis of Israel-Gaza Conflict

There is one curious difference between this news package on Gaza-Israel conflict and the previous news package on the killing of Michael Brown in the United States. In the US-based news package, there was no trace of either the names or the logos of the outside news agencies providing visual footage. In the Israel-Gaza story, however, most logos have not been removed. These include several Middle East-based news agencies.[8] The contrast between the two packages is too sharp to contribute it to poor editing or journalism skills. In the Israel-Gaza case, the logos may have been left on the footage because the original news outlet was in agreement with IRIB's views on the conflict. The logos of Hizbullah- and Hamas-based media are clearly visible, strengthening the theory that the Iranian regime financially supports TV stations and groups affiliated with Hizbullah and Hamas, negating the need for manipulation of the footage (16). The only logo missing from the Israel-Gaza footage is from CNN, a non-Arab/non-Muslim news agency (Figure 5.10, top and bottom images). Here is the context in which the CNN footage has been used

Figure 5.10 The image of Netanyahu from the original footage of the CNN (top) and the image of Netanyahu from CNN footage used by IRIB (bottom).

in two instances. Footage of Netanyahu is shown with the IRIB reporter saying,

> After the mass murder/genocide of the people of Shuja'iyya, the prime minister of the Zionist regime appeared in front of the CNN cameras and said, 'Tel-Aviv only targets the military bases and has nothing to do with women and children.'

The reporter continues, "Netanyahu claims that the resistance groups use people as human shields." "He accused Hamas of not accepting the ceasefire." The word "claim" in this sentence is a metapropositional expressive verb, which marks the IRIB reporter's or the producer's elucidation of Netanyahu's words. That is because claims are not based on facts and can easily be challenged. What the word "claim" is meant to do, however, is to cast a shadow of doubt over what is being said (1). What is withheld here is the conflicting information made available by the United Nations Relief and Works Agency for Palestine Refugees in the Near East. The agency found that Palestinian military ammunition was stored in civilian institutions, which render the buildings non-neutral, hence a target for military attack (17).

Furthermore, the verbs used in the broadcast sentences have connotations. The use of the verb "said" is a neutral structuring verb. This verb is often used to suggest the speaker's—in this case, Netanyahu's—disengagement. The viewer is not encouraged to become personal with Netanyahu in any way. Even though "said" is neutral, other terminological choices made by IRIB producers throughout the text make this verb suggest that Netanyahu's remarks here are unemotional and unattached.

IRIB producers also choose the word "accuse" to express what Netanyahu has said. The word "accuse" is a metapropositional expressive verb. Metapropositional verbs, in general, mean that whoever writes the reports interprets the speaker's words. Thus, when the report says, "He accused Hamas of not accepting the ceasefire," it is the producer's way of saying that Netanyahu believes that Hamas is the one not accepting the ceasefire. Nevertheless, by "accusing" them what Netanyahu is doing—in IRIB's interpretation—is avoiding guilt by connotation. In addition, Netanyahu is shown looking downward, as in Figure 5.10, portraying him as "worried." His gaze is also diverted, meaning that he is not looking directly at the viewer, further underscoring the emotional distance between the viewer and Netanyahu. This type of representation is known as an "offer image," provided for the sole purpose of providing information to the viewer for his/her examination and contemplation (1).

Transitivity Analysis

A transitivity test allowed for the active and passive agents in this news package and their relevant representational words or statements to stand out. With each agent, the related mental, material, behavioral, verbal, relational, and existential processes are also specified. The actors and goals of the processes in this news package are, for the most part, obvious. Israel is an active agent who takes material actions against Palestine and its civilians with material results. Israel "air attacks," it "commits a savage crime," it "destroys residential homes," it "kills"—and the list goes on. The goal is to portray the Palestinians as innocent civilians and the Israelis as aggressors.

The Palestinians, by contrast, are both active and passive agents in this news package. We are told, for example, of a material process of the civilians' preparedness to stand in line with the resistance group. We are privy to the mental processes and reactions of the civilians. We are told about their mourning, grieving, and innocence. Since we are led through the mental processes of these "innocents," we gain access to their state of minds and thus can empathize with them. There are also existential processes at work where the attacks on the civilians have been nominalized, obscuring the agency and responsibility of Palestinian civilians. They are ready to fight but are innocent of any involvement with the conflict. Hence, they are weak agents. The United States, the international community, and the world are also weak agents, as their behavior suggests that they are "cruel," "conspiring," and "supporting," but otherwise ineffectual. In this news package, we are also informed of the material processes of the resistance group, but their actions are justified since they are only in "response to" the attacks initiated by Israel.

There are also visual and verbal processes used in this news package. On two occasions, someone on the side of Israel is given a voice and allowed to "say" something although both times it is used to portray the speaker in a negative light. Netanyahu is given a voice but what he says, as discussed earlier, is a mere "claim." In a second place, we are told, "The Al-Quds Brigades[9] (18) traced and eavesdropped on the two-way radio contact between the Zionists, in which there was a talk about the death of the military personnel." Here again, Israelis are given a chance to speak but the footage leaves the impression that the death of the military personnel was meant to be kept a secret, and the Al-Quds Brigades cunningly find out. The revelation of this secret is confirmed later in the news package, when the viewer is told, "Even with the presence of heavy censorship, the Zionist regime's military has confirmed the death of seven military personnel and the injury of about 60 other of its military personnel. This includes the commander of the Golani Brigade"[10] (19). Outweighing the voice given to the Israelis is that given to Palestine and Palestinian groups, including civilians, resistance groups, and Gaza institutions. In this case, the transitivity is, for the most part, visually represented, allowing the viewer to relate to the Palestinians' inner emotional states.

Lexical Analysis

There are some lexical choices in this news package that replace facts with abstractions and generalizations. In the sentence, "Bodies of tens of women, men, old and young lie in every corner of rubble-stricken streets of Shuja'iyya in the east of Gaza," "tens" is an aggregation, which quantifies participants and treats them as statistics. This use of aggregation gives the impression that there was an objective investigation carried out and the statistics provided here are, therefore, credible (1). In another place, the IRIB reporter says, "Zionists' heavy air, artillery and tank raids, which start every day at dawn, do not even allow for the collection of the mass of corpses." It is not clear what constitutes "heavy," how much is a "mass," or how many "dawns" have witnessed heavy attacks. In another place in the news package, the reporter states, "In response to Israel's attack, the resistance fighters fired hundreds of missiles to Tel-Aviv and different cities of the occupied territories last night and today." Once again, we are not told how many "hundreds" of missiles there are or how many are "different" cities and which ones were involved.

In the chaos of the conflict, an interviewee who seems to be an ambulance driver is shown saying, "All the streets are full of corpses and body parts of martyrs." Here again, "all streets" sounds sizable, but it is still a generalization. How big is Shuja'iyya? How many streets does it have? In other words, how many streets are "all streets"? The IRIB reporter goes on to say, "A deluge of the wounded was flowing towards the hospitals." The word "deluge" is not only a generalization but also a metaphor. It is a flood of the wounded and suggests an overwhelming number of the Palestinian civilians getting injured as a result of the Israeli attacks. Metaphors often hide or redirect true understanding while pretending to reveal it. This metaphor has the effect of magnifying the Israeli attack. In addition, we are not told how many hospitals are meant here and whether some or all are "flooded."

Abstractions continue with the IRIB reporter stating, "Among the dead and the wounded, there are also journalists and aid workers."

Once again, we are not told how many journalists and aid workers are among the casualties. Even though the reporter in one case gives a relatively accurate statistic, saying, "About 70 martyrs and more than 400 wounded are the minimum tolls reported on today's heinous crimes of the Zionists in Shuja'iyya," the generalization and abstraction of the overall information are overlexicalized in this news package. Where abstractions and generalizations take the place of concrete facts, ideology is usually at play. Except for the ambulance driver, the rest of the sentences mentioned earlier do not seem to be quoting anyone—they are the lexical choices made of IRIB producers.

In this news package, certain individuals such as the Gaza Health Ministry Spokesperson, a few civilians, Hamas's spokesperson, Netanyahu, and John Kerry are shown as individuals conveying specific information. At the same time, there is a consistent impersonalization throughout the package to attach further importance to particular statements. For example, in one instance we are told,

> despite requests made by the Red Cross to the international community and official organizations for aiding the wounded in Gaza, not only no response was given to these humanitarian requests, but they [the wounded] were also left to breathe their last breaths.

In this sentence, only whole institutions and groups are mentioned not a particular person. By reporting in such manner, certain issues are concealed. We are not told who from the Red Cross made these requests, who exactly received these requests in the international community, and which official institutions were contacted.

Using grammatical positioning to represent certain events is another linguistic strategy often used for ideological ends. In one instance, for example, the reporter says (translated based on the positioning in the original Persian),

> The prime minister of the Zionist regime, after the mass murder of the people of Shuja'iyya, appeared in front of the cameras of the CNN channel and said 'Tel-Aviv only aims at the military bases and has nothing to do with women and children.'

Here the use of the conjunction "after" makes "the prime minister of the Zionist regime" or Netanyahu the subject of this sentence, and the clause "after the mass murder of the people of Shuja'iyya" is a subordinate clause. The placement of the subordinate clause after introducing the subject leads the viewer to believe that the "prime minister of the Zionist regime" is responsible for the "mass murder." In another place, we are told, "The Zionist regime, in order to complete its crimes, targeted the ambulances as well." In this sentence, once again, the Zionist regime is the subject responsible for all these crimes, including the targeting of ambulances. In the two examples mentioned earlier, because the "Zionist regime" is placed in the main clause, it is the dominant clause and the main focus of what is intended to get across. The killing of women and children and the targeting of the ambulances lose prominence and are played down in order to highlight the actions of the Zionist regime.

A third example also suggests the same. The reporter finishes the news package by saying, "The Zionists' casualties, in spite of the censorship and the anger and fear that have enveloped the occupiers, caused the Zionists in Tel-Aviv and Haifa to hit the streets and to request an end to the war." Once again the "Zionists' casualties" are placed in the dominant clause and made the focus of this sentence. By placing this sentence right at the end of the news package and by positioning the "Zionists' casualties" at the beginning of the sentence before the subordinating conjunction "in spite of," the request of the Israeli people to end the conflict comes across as being not due to their concern for the lives of the Palestinians but rather for the fear of their own lives.

This news package places Israel in an antagonistic position. It is easily understood that Israel is the "enemy," and the sentence structures used to convey it strengthen this point. The Palestinian ordeal is used by IRIB to demonize Israel, an enemy of the regime since 1979 (20–22).

Conclusion

The analysis of the foreign events as presented on IRIB makes Khomeini's definition of collectivity (*ummat*) stand out. Considering the news placement and the extent to which Palestine is covered on television, it seems that IRIB does not consider Palestine a foreign entity. Palestine seems to be considered a part of the *ummat* and the pan-Islamic ideology that Khomeini and subsequently the Iranian regime have been promoting. However, other Islamic countries are not treated the same way. In fact, Iranian laws and regulations obligate the Ministry of Culture and Islamic Guidance and Radio and TV Organization to only "include in their agenda the propaganda support from the Islamic revolution of Palestine," and they have to treat it "as their top overseas priority" (Article 6) (23). This law also prohibits "any economic, commercial and cultural relations with the institutes and companies affiliated with Zionists in any part of the world" (Article 8). Besides this discerning ideology, the analysis of foreign coverage of events, as a whole, points to the fact that the human rights language used by IRIB for reporting purposes is unequivocally clear. Human rights principles are explicitly used to cover international human rights violations of other countries with Israel and the United States being the primary targets.

Notes

1 Functionalization refers to social actors by the roles they play in the society.
2 Nomination employs social actors' unique identity or name.
3 Material processes can be determined asking questions such as "what did the actor do?" and "what happened?"
4 Mir-Hossein Mousavi.
5 The Sabra and Shatila massacres refer to Israel's second invasion of Lebanon, which was launched on June 6, 1982.
6 The Deir Yassin massacre refers to the killing of over 100 Arab civilians by "Jewish paramilitaries" in the British Mandate of Palestine between April 9 and 11, 1948.
7 Additional Protocol II to the Geneva Convention of August 12, 1949, Article 13.3 (adopted on June 8, 1977) (no. 17513).
8 **Al-Aqsa TV Channel**: Hamas's Gaza-based satellite channel; **Al-Manar TV Lebanon** (the beacon): the official television station of the Lebanon-based Hizbullah; **Al-Mayadeen TV Channel**: a Lebanon-based news agency; **Izz ad-Din al-Qassam**: Hamas's military wing in Gaza.
9 The Al-Quds Brigades is another name for the Palestinian Islamic Jihad listed as a terrorist organization.
10 The Golani Brigade is an Israel Defense Forces Unit.

References

1. Machin D, Mayr A. *How to do critical discourse analysis: A multimodal introduction.* London: SAGE; 2012:32, 37, 97, 99, 203.
2. CNN Tonight. *Protests continue in Ferguson; Police in U.S. becoming militarized? (Transcript).* 14 August 2014. Available from: http://transcripts.cnn.com/TRANSCRIPTS/1408/14/cnnt.01.html.
3. UN. *The Universal Declaration of Human Rights.* United Nations General Assembly, editor: [Lake Success]; 1948.
4. AP Television. *US tension.* United States. August 14, 2014. Available from: https://bit.ly/2KrT9OK.
5. JCNews. *Veterans honored with parade, ceremony.* November 9, 2014. Available from: http://myjournalcourier.com/news/home_top-news/50649705/Veterans-honored-with-parade-ceremony.
6. CNN Tonight. *Radley Balko discusses police militarization and the situation in Ferguson, Missouri on CNN Tonight.* 14 August 2014. Available from: http://www.cato.org/multimedia/media-highlights-tv/radley-balko-discusses-police-militarization-situation-ferguson.

7. IranTracker. *Mir-Hossein Mousavi biography and campaign news.* 2009. Available from: http://www.irantracker.org/tehran/mir-hossein-mousavi-biography-and-campaign-news.

8. FardaNews. *Mousavi's instructions on dress code for employees.* June 8, 2009. Available from: https://www.fardanews.com/fa/news/84600/ .نادنمراک-شش‌ووپ-هوحن-هرابرد-یوسوم-روتسد

9. Shahid L. The Sabra and Shatila Massacres: Eye-witness reports. *Journal of Palestine Studies.* 2002;32(1):36.

10. Hogan M. The 1948 Massacre at Deir Yassin revisited. *The Historian.* 2001;63(2):309.

11. Henckaerts J-M, Doswald-Beck L. *Customary International Humanitarian Law: Rules & practices.* (ICRC) ICotRC, editor. New York: Cambridge University Press; 2009:17, 25, 32–4, 79, 98, 115, 193, 406, 568.

12. UN. *Protocol additional to the Geneva Conventions of 12 August 1949, and relating to the protection of victims of non-international armed conflicts (Protocol II).* June 8, 1977. Available from: https://treaties.un.org/doc/Publication/UNTS/Volume 1125/volume-1125-I-17513-English.pdf.

13. Petrig A. The war dead and their gravesites. *International Review of the Red Cross.* 2009;91(874):347

14. van Dijk TA. *Ideology: A multidisciplinary approach.* London: SAGE; 1998:267.

15. ICRC. *International Committee of the Red Cross: Who we are.* 2015. Available from: https://www.icrc.org/en/who-we-are.

16. Jorisch A. *Beacon of hatred: Inside Hizballah's Al-Manar television.* Washington, DC; [Great Britain]: Washington Institute for Near East Policy; 2004.

17. UNRWA. *UNRWA condemns placement of rockets, for a second time, in one of its schools.* 22 July 2014. Available from: http://www.unrwa.org/newsroom/press-releases/unrwa-condemns-placement-rockets-second-time-one-its-schools.

18. ANS. *Palestinian Islamic Jihad.* Australian National Security; 2015. Available from: http://www.nationalsecurity.gov.au/Listedterroristorganisations/Pages/PalestinianIslamicJihad.aspx.

19. IDF. *Israel Defense Forces.* April 30, 2015. Available from: http://www.idf.il/1516-en/Dover.aspx.

20. Khomeini RM. *A collection of the speeches by Imam Khomeini.* Tehran: The Institute for Publication of Imam Khomeini's Works (The Ministry of Islamic Guidance); 1982, Volume 8:235–6.

21. Khomeini RM. *A Collection of the Speeches by Imam Khomeini.* Tehran: The Institute for Publication of Imam Khomeini's Works (The Ministry of Islamic Guidance); 1982, Volume 1:92, 192–4, 144–5, 155, 244.

22. Khomeini RM. *A Collection of the Speeches by Imam Khomeini.* Tehran: The Institute for Publication of Imam Khomeini's Works (The Ministry of Islamic Guidance); 1982, Volume 12:276.

23. Department of Compilation Codification and Publication of Laws and Regulations. *Collection of laws and regulations: Islamic Republic of Iran Broadcasting.* Tehran: Publication and Printing Office; 2015:1031.

6 MCDA of Domestic Events in IRIB News

Introduction

Data in Chapter 4 showed that the coverage of domestic events on Islamic Republic of Iran Broadcasting (IRIB) news is relatively barren of clear human rights language compared to the coverage of foreign affairs. There are, however, enough traces for an in-depth analysis to take place. In this chapter, two domestic news packages are qualitatively analyzed using multimodal critical discourse analysis: one is about a press conference by Judiciary's spokesperson and Iran's Prosecutor General, Gholam-Hossein Mohseni-Eje'i who talks about various issues and the other is about a communication between Sadeq Amoli Larijani, the head of Judiciary, and Khamenei, the Supreme Leader of Iran.

The Judiciary's Press Conference

On August 4, 2014, IRIB released a news package about a press conference by Judiciary's spokesperson and Iran's Prosecutor General, Gholam-Hossein Mohseni-Eje'i. The IRIB anchor, Mohammad-Reza Hayati, seems calm and composed, and he opens with "Judicial news from the spokesperson." "In this meeting,

> Hujjatul-Islām wa l-Muslimīn[1] (1) Mohseni-Eje'i, Prosecutor General of Iran, while addressing the execution of three miscreants in Shiraz, said 'the strategy of the Judiciary is to deal decisively with those who violate the life, property, and reputation of others.'"

Besides the executions, the spokesperson also addressed a host of other issues:

1   The implementation of the "dignity of women" project in the municipality.
2   Latest Zionist crimes in Gaza.

3 Environmental pollution.
4 Conviction in absentia of seditionists[2] (2).
5 Confrontation with various offenders inside the Judiciary.
6 The arrest of individuals associated with illegal satellite channels.
7 Special courts for complaints against crimes of the United States.

**The Judiciary Report and the International Human
Rights Law**

Each of the earlier issues addressed by Mohseni-Eje'i is associated
with international human rights principles, humanitarian laws, or *jus
cogens*. The in-depth analysis in this chapter will show how they are
portrayed by IRIB and for what purposes.

Executions in the City of Shiraz

As already stated, Iran is party to both the International Covenant
on Civil and Political Rights (ICCPR) and the Universal Declaration
of Human Rights (UDHR) and hence bound by all their provisions.
UDHR is a non-binding international legal instrument containing the
basic, fundamental rights of everyone (3). Article 6(2) of ICCPR states
that "In countries which have not abolished the death penalty, a sentence of death may be imposed only for the most serious crimes in
accordance with the law in force at the time of the commission of the
crime" (4). The Human Rights Committee, which has the authority to
interpret this covenant, limits the use of the death penalty to "quite
exceptional measure" (5). In this news report, IRIB provides no information on the three executed "miscreants" or the nature of their
crimes. Thus, the viewer cannot tell from the package whether any
international rules, such as juvenile executions (6), have been violated.
It is unclear whether these individuals were given the right to seek pardon, clemency, reprieve, or commutation as specifically called for in
Article 6(4) of the ICCPR (4).

"Dignity of Women" Project

A little research on the implementation of "dignity of women" project
in municipalities shows that it is a gender-segregation initiative. "The
initiative separates men and women's offices in the municipality and
limits women's access to managerial and clerical positions" (7). As a
result, all women in managerial and clerical positions are to be replaced
by males to regulate their presence in the public sphere. In the news
package, Mohseni-Eje'i is quoted as saying, "this measure has been

implemented in the prosecutor's office, and everyone must support the municipality's actions." While Iran is party to five core instruments, it has so far refused to sign the Convention on the Elimination of All Forms of Discrimination Against Women. However, there are other international instruments on human rights and equality of the genders that Iran is party to. Article 2 of the UDHR states, "Everyone is entitled to all the rights and freedoms set forth in this Declaration, without distinction of any kind, such as ... sex..." (8). Article 2(1) of ICCPR states,

> Each State Party to the present Covenant undertakes to respect and to ensure to all individuals within its territory and subject to its jurisdiction the rights recognized in the present Covenant, without distinction of any kind, such as ... sex... (4)

Environmental Issues

Environmental issues—pollution, deforestation, illegal construction, destruction of rivers, and unauthorized issuance of decrees for the destruction of properties—are among the topics that Mohseni-Eje'i brings up but he only "hopes" that the different organs of the regime would start "cooperating." Article 50 of the Iranian Constitution states,

> The preservation of the environment, in which the present, as well as the future generations, have a right to flourishing social existence, is regarded as a public duty in the Islamic Republic. Economic and other activities that inevitably involve pollution of the environment or cause irreparable damage to it are therefore forbidden (9).

In this news package, the information about which government agencies are involved with the aforementioned environmental issues is withheld. Internationally, Iran is also party to a host of treaties, instruments, and conventions that support the preservation of the environment. There are, however, no indications that Mohseni-Eje'i would take any actions in prosecuting those involved with the environmental issues.

Conviction in Absentia of Seditionists

Regarding the case of the "seditionists," Mohseni-Eje'i reports to have dealt, in absentia, with the charges of 38 individuals accused of sedition. Article 10 of the UDHR states, "Everyone is entitled in full equality to a fair and public hearing by an independent and impartial tribunal, in the determination of his rights and obligations and of any criminal charge against him" (8). In addition, Article 14 of the ICCPR lays out the processes for persons accused of crimes:

1 All persons shall be equal before the courts and tribunals. In the determination of any criminal charge against him, or of his rights and obligations in a suit at law, everyone shall be entitled to a fair and public hearing by a competent, independent, and impartial tribunal established by law. ...

2 Everyone charged with a criminal offense shall have the right to be presumed innocent until proved guilty according to law.

3 In the determination of any criminal charge against him, everyone shall be entitled to the following minimum guarantees, in full equality:

    a To be informed promptly and in detail in a language which he understands of the nature and cause of the charge against him;

    b To have adequate time and facilities for the preparation of his defence and to communicate with counsel of his own choosing;

    c To be tried without undue delay;

    d To be tried in his presence, and to defend himself in person or through legal assistance of his own choosing; to be informed, if he does not have legal assistance, of this right; and to have legal assistance assigned to him, in any case where the interests of justice so require, and without payment by him in any such case if he does not have sufficient means to pay for it;

    ...

5 Everyone convicted of a crime shall have the right to his conviction and sentence being reviewed by a higher tribunal according to law.

    ...

In the sedition cases, we are not told whether these individuals are juveniles, and we are not told whether they had any legal assistance. However, we are explicitly told that they were not present at the time of their convictions, thus violating Article 14.3(d) of the ICCPR.

Article 14 also requires the court to be independent. However, as was illustrated in Chapter 3, the Supreme Leader of Iran appoints the head of the Judiciary. The head of the Judiciary, in turn, appoints the head of the Supreme Court and the chief public prosecutor (10). Since the Judiciary and the courts are entirely entangled with the political system, this violation of the international human rights law is not an oversight but rather a deliberate and systematic exertion of power by the Islamic Republic of Iran.

Confrontation with Various Offenders Inside the Judiciary

The next point raised by Mohseni-Eje'i concerns the conviction of three judges and ten lawyers and the prosecution of many more. Their identities, the details of the nature of their convictions, their crimes, legal proceedings, access to lawyers, the nature of the trials, and appeal processes are all withheld. These absences may be because either the Judiciary or the news producer did not wish the viewers to consider them. It is clear that the human rights language used in this news package is purposefully vague and nonspecific, allowing the speaker to dismiss any questions that might arise about the accused and their rights.

The Arrest of Individuals in Connection with the Ownership of Illegal Satellite Channels

Mohseni-Eje'i then raises another point about the arrest of "a number of individuals in connection with the ownership of illegal satellite channels." He is quoted to say, "They published materials against Islam. They were dealt with in a few provinces. A few of the main agents were arrested. They are in custody now. Their illegal offices have been shut down." Article 9(1) of ICCPR emphasizes,

> Everyone has the right to liberty and security of person. No one shall be subjected to arbitrary arrest or detention. No one shall be deprived of his liberty except on such grounds and in accordance with such procedure as are established by law (8).

Iranian law divides the country into public, cooperative, and private sectors. However, as stated in Article 44 of the Constitution, radio and television, post, telegraph, and telephone are considered "public property and at the disposal of the Government" (9). This is while the Iranian regime has signed and ratified the UDHR, which states, "Everyone has the right to freedom of opinion and expression; this right includes freedom to hold opinions without interference and to seek, receive and impart information and ideas through any media and regardless of frontiers" (Article 19).

Lexical and Visual Analysis

Moving on from the legal aspect of the points raised in the news, the connotations of the words used with regard to the implementation of the law are of interest as well. A few examples are the use of the word "miscreant"[3] for the people who have been executed or the use of the word "violated"[4] for those who have infringed on the rights of others and the use of the word "sedition"[5] for those who have been accused of wrongdoing. These words in Persian convey heinous crimes, but we are not told what they mean and what these individuals have exactly done to be categorized as such. This is not explicitly stated but the words—"miscreant," "violation," and "sedition"—have clear negative connotations. If these individuals are "miscreants" and "violators," it is understood that they have acted in a manner opposed to what is expected of a good citizen or member of the community, an example of ideological squaring, discussed in Chapter 5.

The lexical choices and the repeated warnings of the Prosecutor General for the people to take heed against "miscreant groups" intentionally legitimize the executions and arbitrary arrests. The visual and lexical information that might allow the viewer to be informed of the situation is also withheld. We know virtually nothing about the accused individual. Indeed, there is a noticeable departure from the bombardment of visual and verbal information about the Israel and Gaza conflict discussed in Chapter 5. Logically, internal information should be more easily obtainable.

The visual choices are also kept very simple in this news package. We are only shown the IRIB anchor, a reporter at the press conference, Hasan Yousofi from Central News Unit, and scenes from the press conference, with a particular focus on Mohseni-Eje'i (Figure 6.1).

Figure 6.1 Shots from a press conference with Mohseni-Eje'i, Prosecutor General of Iran.

The news footage denotes a room filled with reporters in rectangular seating positions either filming the proceedings, listening, or recording information from the press conference. Mohseni-Eje'i is positioned at the head of this configuration, suggesting his higher status (Figure 6.1, bottom left) (11). Mohseni-Eje'i's black cloak and white turban connote his religious authority as belonging to 'ulama (12).[6] On the wall behind Mohseni-Eje'i are two photos of the current and former Supreme Leaders, Khamenei and Khomeini. There are also two flags, one of the Islamic Republic of Iran (on the right-hand side of Mohseni-Eje'i) and the other of the Judiciary Power of the Islamic Republic of Iran (on the left-hand side of Mohseni-Eje'i). The flags, along with the photos of the Supreme Leaders, underscore the immense politico-religious significance and importance of Mohseni-Eje'i's statements. All the visual representations in the news package convey political and religious ideologies and carry particular symbolisms that the target audience will understand.

Throughout this news report, there is a predominance use and overlexicalization of the terms "deal" with criminals, "arrests," "implementation" of "laws" and projects, and certain "actions" and "measures." None of these words are surprising, given that the spokesperson is the Prosecutor General of Iran. At the same time, the overuse of these terms indicates anxiety on the part of Mohseni-Eje'i and IRIB, who see them as necessary for justifying the executions, prosecutions, and arrests of individuals who are supposedly endangering the community.

What are not expected in this package are Mohseni-Eje'i's comments on the Israel-Gaza conflict in his opening statement:

> Unfortunately, this illegitimate Occupier and the murderous regime continues with its crimes and the killing of women and children. Also, unfortunately, the international community and some Arab countries do not take any appropriate and worthy measures against such criminal acts.

These comments are irrelevant to Mohseni-Eje'i's duties as the second-highest official in the judicial system, but the Israel-Gaza conflict seems to be reinforced wherever possible.

Another unexpected statement made by the Prosecutor General is his mention of special courts that handle complaints against the Americans for their crimes. Throwing in mentions of Israel and the United States in a judicial press conference encourages viewers to link the two countries to the "miscreants" and "violators" in this news report and hence elicit similar feelings of repulsion and hatred.

The verbs used in this news package are also significant. Five quoting verbs—"announced" (assertive), "informed" (assertive), "said" (neutral), "pointed out" (assertive), and "requested/urged" (directive)—are used repetitively throughout the package. While the neutral structuring verb "said" introduces some of Mohseni-Eje'i's statements without evaluation, the other verbs are metapropositional and represent the reporter's interpretation of the press conference. Thus, in the context of this package, Mohseni-Eje'i comes across as an informed and reliable individual whose words have a bearing on the judicial system (13).

Visual Cues and Power Relations

Besides the lexical choices made concerning Mohseni-Eje'i, he is visually presented in a few different ways (Figure 6.2). In most instances, he is shown in a close-up shot with his gaze toward the viewer. His face is expressionless, and his tone is calm. Except for occasional movements of the head, he is very still and self-contained. His direct gaze at the viewer creates a bond between them (13). This gaze frames his two requests of the people and families. He uses a directive verb to demand people's cooperation. However, by requesting something from the people he is using a lowered modality, which lets him come across as sincere (13). In these two instances, Mohseni-Eje'i communicates his moral position

Figure 6.2 Different shots of Mohseni-Eje'i shown in the coverage of the press conference.

while admitting the viewers into his inner world (13). In general, what politicians try to do is to profess in both being "certain" and "decisive" while still being "approachable" and "humane" (13). In one instance, for example, the IRIB anchor states, "referring to the implementation of women's dignity project in municipalities, the Prosecutor General said, 'this measure has been implemented in the Prosecutor's Office as well, and everyone *must* support the municipality's actions.'" The use of the deontic modal "must" asserts Mohseni-Eje'i's certainty and confidence in his directive. Looking directly at the camera also conveys that the issues are being dealt with straight on. However, he is also shown at the same height as the viewer, suggesting that he is an ordinary person.

In some instances, Mohseni-Eje'i is also shown looking off the frame. This invites the viewer to imagine what he is thinking. His head and gaze are tilted upward, and he has an upward gaze. This represents Mohseni-Eje'i positively, which is often the case with politicians who are shown looking off the frame and slightly upward. The side view in combination with the close-up shot may also portray Mohseni-Eje'i's togetherness and encourages the viewers to align their thoughts and concerns with him.

In addition, Mohseni-Eje'i is both nominated and functionalized throughout the news package. For instance, the report starts with Mohseni-Eje'i's full honorific: Hujjatul-Islām wa l-Muslimīn Mohseni-Eje'i. The use of his honorific conveys the importance of his social role and his authoritativeness, which requires a degree of respect and obedience. Since other social actors are not visually represented in this news package, no visual semiotic resources can be used to analyze them. There are only Mohseni-Eje'i's statements to consider.

The Representational Strategies of Social Actors

Going back to Mohseni-Eje'i's statements, it is important to shed light on the representational strategies used to portray each social actor mentioned in the news. Three individuals who were executed are represented as "miscreants." The "otherness" of these individuals is emphasized to show that they are a "problem" (13). Since these individuals were born in Iran, Mohseni-Eje'i could have stated that three Iranian citizens or simply three citizens were executed. However, that would have meant that these three individuals were "one of us." In general, the creation of moral otherness has become the norm when it comes to reporting on crimes. This is done so to avoid presenting the perpetrator as one of "us" and to make sure s/he is categorized as the enemy (13). This is a clear example of antagonism, discussed in Chapter 2. By creating opposites and aligning the viewers against the three executed individuals, the issue is simplified and its meaning controlled.

The mention of "miscreants" and "miscreant groups" comes up again later in the report where the reporter says, "regarding the seriousness of the Judiciary system towards miscreants, the Prosecutor General urged the families to look out for miscreant groups especially those involved with drugs." This is the only reference given to what Mohseni-Eje'i may mean by "miscreant." By warning people against miscreants and driving the miscreants to their ultimate destiny— execution—a certain moral panic is created. However, because of the extreme abstraction and vagueness, the moral panic is created against an "imaginary enemy," which could potentially include many people.

The increase in executions in Iran from 2004 to 2015 (Figure 6.3)[7] suggests the disintegration of the authoritative religious structure and the outdated social order in Iran (14–17). The underlying hardships and stresses of the society and whether the executed individuals were from deprived backgrounds with many social problems are withheld in this news package. The number of executions in Iran has declined slightly since 2016 due to changes in Iran's drug-trafficking laws, but it still has the highest number of recorded executions in the world after China (18).

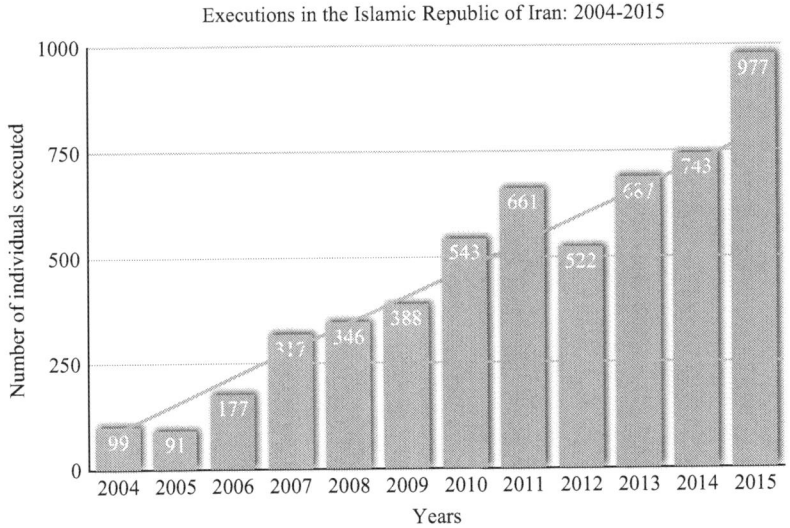

Executions in the Islamic Republic of Iran: 2004-2015

Figure 6.3 Confirmed executions in the Islamic Republic of Iran from 2004 to 2015.

Not naming the "miscreants" attaches more importance to Mohseni-Eje'i's statement (13). It is not just three individuals that need to be dealt with, but a whole lot of them. This generalization conceals issues such as poverty. By grouping these individuals into one, they become part of a collectivity and therefore generic. Consequently, the viewers have no way of identifying with them.

The suppression of information is also evident in other statements made by Mohseni-Eje'i. Regarding the environmental issues, for example, he says, "We are hopeful that coordination between the environment and other organs would take place. Sometimes a state organization issues a warrant without seeking the opinion of the environment." In this sentence, the agents are missing. The environment is not something that can either coordinate or be consulted with. The report conceals who is ultimately responsible for taking environmental action.

Transitivity Test

A transitivity test of the text illuminates how different actors are being represented in this news package. Out of the eight participants represented in this package—Mohseni-Eje'i, miscreants/criminals/seditionists, Zionists, environment/government organizations, families/people, Judiciary, Americans, and "some" Arab countries—only the first two are given agency through mental or material processes (actions). However, the actions of the miscreants/criminals/seditionists are portrayed negatively. The actions of miscreants include drug offenses[8] (19) and "violations" of life, property, and reputation of people and families. People and families are participants against whom these actions are supposedly taken but as passive actors. They must be careful and cautious. The families and people are thus encouraged to be active only in their behavioral and mental processes.

Meanwhile, the actions of criminals are indicated to be publications against Islam and the actions of seditionists are said to be activities against the government, as is also implied in the word seditionist. Therefore, Islam and the Iranian regime are passive participants of such actions. Mohseni-Eje'i and the Judiciary also take action through material processes, but this time their passive agents are miscreants, criminals, and seditionists who are convicted, prosecuted, and arrested. The Judiciary's actions are portrayed as good since miscreants, criminals, and seditionists have already been established as bad people who must be punished. Another difference between these two groups, i.e. Mohseni-Eje'i and the miscreants/criminals/seditionists, is that Mohseni-Eje'i goes through a mental process as well. This means that the viewers only gain insight into the feelings and the state of mind of Mohseni-Eje'i but not the miscreants, criminals, or seditionists. For example, Mohseni-Eje'i "hopes," "supports," and "urges" while the viewers are left with no mental cues from miscreants, criminals, and seditionists.

In this news package, Mohseni-Eje'i also goes through a verbal process. He is the only participant who is given a voice. Mohseni-Eje'i's material processes, combined with his representation as the doer of material processes on miscreants, criminals, and seditionists, make him a powerful figure. This is in contrast to "some Arab countries" that are represented as not taking appropriate actions in relation to the Israel/Palestine conflict, rendering them weak agents. This is also called hedging as the use of the term "some" in association with Arab countries creates "strategic ambiguity" within Mohseni-Eje'i's claim. By doing so, Mohseni-Eje'i evades being direct while giving the impression of being specific and to the point (13).

By looking at the grammatical positioning of actions, it becomes clear that convicts are divided into two groups: those who are ordinary people and those who are from within the Judiciary itself. In the case of ordinary people, the viewers are told what precisely their verdicts are. They are either imprisoned or executed. However, in the case of Judiciary employees, the audiences are not told about the nature of their convictions. The viewers are just told that they were convicted in a way that downplays the convictions and emphasizes the prosecutions. For example, at one point, the reporter states that "up until now eight judges have been prosecuted, three of whom have been convicted." In the second instance, it is stated, "Out of the 12 lawyers who were prosecuted, for 10 of them, verdicts have been issued." The grammatical positioning and the use of the passive voice in both sentences render the cases of the Judiciary employees ambiguous since the viewers are not told what these judges and lawyers have done to warrant prosecution. The news package, however, fuels Mohseni-Eje'i's claim that there are serious issues within the Judiciary.

This news package is compressed with events and filled with nominalizations or concealments, both linguistically and visually. In addition, there is no sense of time with any of the events mentioned in the news. The manner in which various events are condensed makes the solutions seem reasonable and feasible (13). There are also certain presuppositions in this news package, which are "assumed as given" (13). For example, Mohseni-Eje'i is reported to say, "They [a group of criminals] published materials against Islam." This explanation is vague as well as ideological because it lacks definition and completely ignores freedom of expression. The audience is not told what was published, and it is assumed that everyone knows what constitutes Islam despite the variety that exists within the faith. The assumption is that if everyone accepts that there is one true Islam, as dictated by the Islamic Republic of Iran, then it is easier to persuade the public that Islam is in need of protection (13) and whoever is not part of this religion or expresses anything contradictory is a criminal.

The Supreme Leader's Clemency or Commutation of Punishments on the Occasion of Eid-e Fetr

This domestic news package was broadcast on July 27, 2014 as part of a one-hour program. The anchor of this news package is Reza Hosseinzadeh. He starts the news by reading "Clemency or commutation of punishments of a group convicted by the courts on the occasion of Eid-e Fetr." The package concerns a letter written by Sadeq Amoli Larijani, the head of Judiciary, to Iran's Supreme Leader, Khamenei, and Khamenei's response to Larijani.

Lexical Analysis

The news package is quite simple, both in terms of the producer's report and visual semiotics. However, the heavy use of legal terms and official-sounding lexical semiotics creates a complex authoritative and official legal effect. Except for the title, the anchor only has one more line. The rest of the news package is a direct reading of Larijani's letter to Khamenei and Khamenei's response. The anchor's second line is

> His Excellency Ayatollah Khamenei, the Supreme Leader of the Islamic Revolution, at the request of Ayatollah Amoli Larijani, the head of Judiciary, and on the occasion of Eid-e Fetr, agreed to the terms and conditions of clemency or commutation of punishments of inmates convicted by either the Public and Revolutionary Courts (20), the State Discretionary Punishment Organization (21, 22),[9] or the Judicial Organization of the Armed Forces (23, 24).[10]

The anchor then goes on to read the content of Larijani's letter, followed by Khamenei's response. In contrast to the previous news packages, this news package is loaded with legal terms and references to Islamic criminal and penal codes. What immediately stands out is the non-derogable law in Article 6(4) of the ICCPR, which obliges the state parties to provide "the right to seek pardon or commutation of the sentence" by those who have been condemned to death (4, 25). However, in Larijani's letter to Khamenei, the death sentence is not listed as eligible for clemency or commutation. Only those sentenced to prison or fined penalty charges are listed as eligible for appeal. Even then, Larijani's request for clemency and commutation on the convicts' behalf is not due to human rights but rather due to "Islamic compassion," which is bestowed by the Supreme Leader.

"Islamic compassion" is an interesting lexical choice. First of all, it is not defined. When a concept is used without definition, it is usually deeply ideological. The Islamic compassion is supposedly bestowed only to certain groups, which does not include the perpetrators of the following crimes:

1 Armed robbery or aggravated assault or robbers whose convictions of imprisonment are more than five years.
2 Armed or organized drug trafficking (what is meant by drug trafficking is crimes in Article 4(4), Article 5(6), and Article 8(6) of Anti-Narcotic Law and related drugs).
3 Arms and ammunition smuggling.
4 Acts against internal and external security.
5 Abduction.
6 Rape.
7 Establishment of centers of corruption and prostitution.
8 Bribery and embezzlement.
9 Paper money forgery and coin counterfeiting.
10 Acid attack.
11 Crimes related to alcoholic drinks.

All other groups must have served a percentage of their prison term in order to be eligible for the mercy of the Islamic state. Based on the statistics from the International Centre for Prison Studies, the total number of detainees, including remanded prisoners, was 225,624 in December 2014 (26). Out of these, 25.1% were remanded prisoners. In this news package, there is no mention of remanded prisoners. Therefore, 25.1% (56,631) of the prisoners are not eligible for clemency or commutation. That leaves 168,993 individuals who may be eligible. However, according to a report dated October 11, 2014, by PressTV, clemency and commutation applied to only 1,256 individuals (21). That leaves 167,737 prisoners who either did not qualify or belong to one of the above 11 excluded categories. It must be noted that PressTV is also state-owned and no other official sources could be found to confirm the number of individuals who were either released or whose convictions were commuted.

One category of the 11 excluded from clemency in Larijani's letter is particularly vague. Category four includes prisoners who were convicted of "acts against the internal and external security" of the nation or Islam. This is an abstraction and a generalization that could potentially include political prisoners, journalists, religious and ethnic minority groups, and lawyers. A whole array of the principles of international human rights law such as minority and ethnic rights, freedom of speech, and freedom of the press might be relevant if the details of what constitutes an act against national security were not suppressed. This might be why this information has been suppressed.

With regard to convicts, there is no mention of the nature of their crimes, just types of convictions. The heavy focus on the convictions and the convoluted legal calculations of eligibility for clemency and commutation do not allow for consideration of other legal matters such as whether these individuals were arbitrarily arrested, whether they had access to independent lawyers, whether they had a fair trial, whether they were convicted justly, whether their convictions reflected the nature of their crimes, and whether they were kept under humane conditions in prison. These individuals have not been given a voice, and they have not been named or visually represented. This may be because the intention of this news package is not to foreground the convicts but rather to place the Supreme Leader on the center stage. It is clear that the viewers are not meant to get close and intimate with these convicts. They are, however, encouraged to get closer to their leader who is visually presented with a positive, contemplative smile, presumably as part of the mission to demonstrate the Islamic compassion (Figure 6.4).

Figure 6.4 A shot of the IRIB anchor, Reza Hosseinzadeh with a large picture of Iran's Supreme Leader, Ayatollah Khamenei.

Visual Analysis

This picture of Khamenei appears early on in the news package. He is shown in the background as the anchor briefly summarizes the two letters. Even though Khamenei's photo is in the background, it appears much larger than the anchor. Khamenei is shown in a close-up but in profile, which could suggest togetherness. His gaze is to the distance and portrays him as thoughtful, inviting the viewer to imagine what he is thinking. Because he is not looking straight at the viewers, instead of acknowledging them and seeking a reaction, the image is offered to the viewers for their contemplation and examination (13). Khamenei is wearing a black turban, representing his relation to Prophet Muhammad hence the honorific title "Sayyid," which Khamenei employs at the end of his response to Larijani. He is also wearing a black cloak and what is called a *keffiyeh* around his neck. *Keffiyeh* is an iconography of a black and white-chequered scarf, which is suggested to be a "symbol of resistance in Palestine." It is Khamenei's way of commemorating the religious war in which Iranian forces fought for eight years against the Iraqis (27, 28). The flag of the Islamic Republic of Iran is also shown alongside Khamenei.

All these elements are salient in one way or another. Certain features stand out to foreground specific meanings. Khamenei's attire, especially his black turban and his *keffiyeh*, are potent cultural symbols. With the addition of the flag, they symbolize religion and politics in Iran. The size of Khamenei's photo indicates his importance. Khamenei's background is blurred, further highlighting his person. With the lowered visual modality and decreased articulation of the background, the image loses its origin in space and time because the focus is not when and where this photo was taken but rather who Khamenei is. Once again, the background is less saturated and therefore muted. Khamenei, on the other hand, is perfectly in focus. Thus, his face stands out against the background. There is also certain brightness on Khamenei's face, which draws attention to his eyes. Foregrounding Khamenei against the muted background enhances his stature and importance. Furthermore, overlapping, which is a technique used for foregrounding, gives the impression that Khamenei is not only overshadowing the blurred background but also the Iranian flag. He is, therefore, presented as more important than the national flag.

Further Lexical Analysis

Further lexical analysis of the text shows that there are only three verbs used in this news package: "request," "agree," and "approve." Larijani "requests." Khamenei "agrees" and "approves." "Request" is a directive metapropositional verb and, in the context of the news package, gives the impression of an appeal rather than a simple request. Larijani appeals for Islamic compassion from the highest religious and political authority, which Larijani acknowledges in the Arabic phrase, "the command is yours," that ends his letter. Khamenei, in turn, agrees and accepts. By using assertive metapropositional verbs, Khamenei establishes his agency and authority. His short response to Larijani indicates that he has no objection with what Larijani is proposing. They are united on the topic. This is curiously illustrated in a subsequent image from the news package where Khamenei has been reduced from a looming figure (Figure 6.4) to the same size as Larijani (Figure 6.5).

Even though Khamenei has the final say, this image equalization suggests that the Iranian regime, as a whole, is compassionate and merciful toward its nation. Both Khamenei and Larijani are relaxed, composed, and self-contained. In Figure 6.5, both Larijani and Khamenei are shown in close-up and looking directly at the viewer. The photographs have been cropped to take the viewer closer to the two men, allowing the viewer into their inner states and feelings. This has a twofold effect. First, the men in the images seemingly acknowledge and engage with the viewer. Second, the images seem to call for some reaction from the viewer in this imaginary relationship between the public and the state. There are no clear emotions on either man's face except for a slight smile on Khamenei's face. However,

Figure 6.5 An image of Larijani and Khamenei shown beside each other.

by acknowledging the viewers, there is a sense that the state and the authorities are more accessible to the public. Since both Larijani and Khamenei are acknowledging the existence of the viewer, they seem to invite the viewer to identify with and be like them. The close-up combined with the straight-on gaze suggests they are open and sincere. Further, the bright background and occasional highlights over the two men's heads suggest optimism and hope. The iconographical features and lexical semiotic choices encourage the viewers to find salvation and ultimate happiness through their political and religious guardians.

The lexical choices used in this news package to classify the social actors are also of interest. The convicts are impersonalized. The title of the news package is "Clemency or commutation of punishments of a group convicted by the courts on the occasion of Eid-e Fetr." Thus, there are no particular individuals but a "group" of them. This technique conceals exactly who is being released and whose convictions are being reduced. There is also collectivization of the individuals. They are a "group of convicts," "those convicted," "those condemned," and "perpetrators"—all generic labels. On the other hand, Larijani and Khamenei are humanized, in stark contrast to the convicts.

Larijani and Khamenei are also both functionalized and nominated. The use of functionalization makes this news package sound more official while the nomination makes it sound personal. Both Khamenei and Larijani are functionalized as "Ayatollah." In the case of Khamenei, further functional honorifics, "His Excellency" and "the Supreme Leader of the Islamic Revolution," are used. These functional honorifics highlight Khamenei's importance. In his response to Larijani, Khamenei does not use an opening line to address him, and by not using a functional honorific to address Larijani, Larijani's authority is diminished compared to Khamenei's. This is yet another strategy to emphasize Khamenei's authority.

Transitivity Test

Three groups—Khamenei, Larijani, and state organizations[11]— are part of the state apparatus and are thus active agents in this news story. Khamenei "agrees" and "approves." Both of these terms suggest material processes with Larijani as the recipient and the convicts as the beneficiaries. Larijani's "request" and his setting of "terms and conditions" are also material processes with Khamenei as the goal and the convicts as the beneficiaries. The fourth group consists of Public and Revolutionary Courts, the State Discretionary Punishment Organization, and the Judicial Organization of Armed Forces, who convict individuals based on their crimes. Individuals' convictions are also material processes with the convicts as the receptors of the courts' actions. The convicts, on the other hand, are passive participants with no active role. The convicts go through existential processes because they have spent time in jail or have endured imprisonment; yet their actions have not been voluntary. They were not imprisoned because they were powerful but because they were powerless. There is only one glimpse of agency in Larijani's letter, and that is of the women convicts, eligible for clemency, who have custody of their children. However, even this slight agency is quickly diminished since these women have custody of their children not because they are the biological parents but because the law has awarded custody to them.

What is interesting is that even the convicts have a hierarchy regarding their level of agencies. For example, because of the grammatical positioning of actions in the following group in Larijani's letter, the alien nationals are represented as having even a weaker agency than other convicts:

> The remainder of the conviction of imprisonment and the monetary charges of male convicts over 65 years of age and females over 55 years of age based on legal records and for alien nationals without legal documents, based on verification of Legal Medicine Provincial Branches. This is on the condition that in the case of conviction of imprisonment over one year, a minimum of one fifth, and in the case of life imprisonment, a minimum of five years has been endured.

The convicts are also not visually represented as agents, contributing to their weakness. The only visual cue the viewer has is the infographic listing of the different groups eligible for clemency and commutation (Figure 6.6).

On the headline banner of each infographic, there is a summary of the news, which reads: "Agreement with clemency and commutation of convicts' punishments" and at the bottom, the terms and conditions are laid out. This is an "ideal-real" composition where the top-bottom arrangement has a potential meaning. The top is usually the ideal and the bottom is the real. By placing the terms and conditions at the bottom, a greater gravity is given to them (29). However, the use of color, font, and alignment in the context of the whole news package places more importance on the top banner—which emphasizes Islamic compassion—especially because it is repeated on every slide.

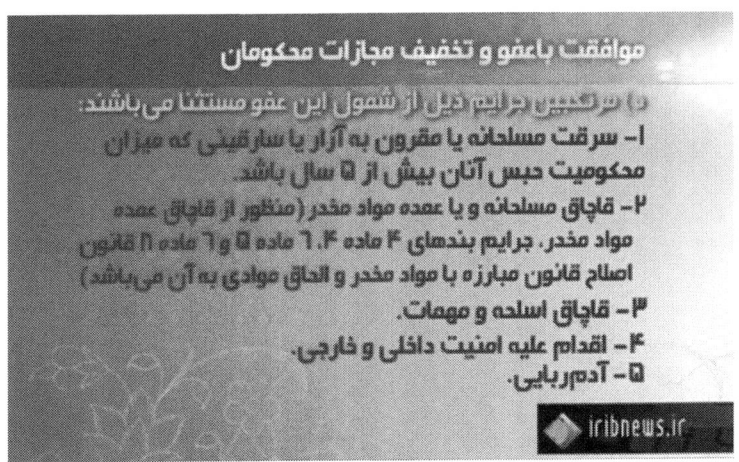

Figure 6.6 Infographics of the list of those eligible for clemency and commutation based on Larijani's letter.

The font color of the headlines in the top banner is white against a light to dark saturated blue background. Blue is often associated with "openness, peace, and tranquility" (30). In addition, in Iranian culture, blue is also associated with depth and stability. It is a symbol of reality and truth, loyalty and honesty, intelligence and wisdom, confidence and generosity, and ultimately paradise (31). The white font color at the top represents light, purity, goodness, and optimism. The bright light on the right-hand corner of the infographics visually adds to this connotation. White also connotes security (31).

The body of the infographic consists of group titles in yellow and a list of related items in dark blue. Yellow is associated with the sun and therefore connotes warmth, kindness, and happiness. As Figure 6.6 illustrates, the texts are aligned on the right-hand side but are ragged on the left.[12] This sort of arrangement looks more "organic" and allows the words to take as much space as needed (29). The text appears "natural" and "relaxed," but because each line ends up at a different position, it makes it difficult to read. Such alignment makes the texts appear less formal but at the same time connotes confidence.

Even though each infographic has large borders on three sides (right, left, and bottom), which connotes open-mindedness and luxury, the line spacing is limited. This narrow line spacing connotes that the elements are tightly connected. The font has been kept the same for all infographics, both for the title and the content of the letter.

Such regularity conveys formality. Even the font size and weight of the letters are kept the same, which maintains consistency and connotes uniformity in eminence or worth (29). The font also appears curved. Curvature connotes smoothness, softness, and gentleness. It is organic in character. In the context of the news package, the aforementioned connotations are not meant to be directed at the convicts but rather at Khamenei, who is shown once again at the end of the news package with the anchor reading his response to Larijani (Figure 6.7).

Khamenei is shown once again against a blue background with beautiful calligraphy of the Islamic phrase "In the name of God, the

Figure 6.7 Images of Khamenei shown at the end of news package during the reading of his response to Larijani.

Most Gracious, the Most Merciful" in Arabic. The calligraphy, then, changes to the flag of the Islamic Republic of Iran. Both the Arabic script from the Quran and the flag reiterate Khamenei's lineage and authority and emphasize his power and position.

Conclusion

It is clear from the data and the analysis of the two domestic news packages discussed in this chapter that the human rights language is very vague when it comes to IRIB's coverage of domestic affairs. Since the opposite was true with IRIB's coverage of foreign news events examined in Chapter 5, the lack of clear human rights language in domestic news is undoubtedly intentional. Even though the human rights language is clear in the reportage of foreign events, the intention does not seem to be the promotion of human rights principles or the international human rights norms. It is rather the creation of antagonism toward certain states that are "enemies" of the Islamic Republic of Iran. The photos, images, and footages borrowed from foreign news agencies are also used selectively to manipulate the information for political ends. Domestic news lacks the human rights language altogether, and the suppression of information against victims of human rights violations, and the use of broad criminal terms against them seem to, once again, be a tactic for a political end, which is to gain legitimacy from the people. Therefore, the human rights climate that the Iranian delegation to the United Nations (UN) says Iran is creating is nothing but a further violation of the international human rights law on the part of the state.

The data show that the Islamic Republic seeks legitimacy through the representation of a positive self. This strategy is used by the Iranian regime as a means of representing the Supreme Leader and the "system" as generous, forgiving, and God-sent. This could be taken as an oxymoron to the regime's relationship with the rest of the world and its mentality toward the West. An example is the regime's relationship with the UN. The Islamic Republic, for instance, has not opted out of the UN and continues to report to its mechanisms, hence giving it legitimacy. However, the regime painstakingly questions the UN's authority or legitimacy at every opportunity (32).

Notes

1 Hujjatul-Islām wa l-Muslimīn means "Authority on Islam and Muslims." It was originally an honorific given to Shi'ite scholars. However, today it is also indicative of their "status in the hierarchy of the learned."
2 In the Iranian conservative media, "seditionists" refer to those individuals who were involved in the 2009 post-election Green Movement protests.

3 شرور
4 تعدی
5 فتنه

6 The white turban distinguishes him from those who wear black. Those mullahs who are descendants of the Prophet Muhammad wear a black turban.

7 The figure includes both official and semiofficial government sources in addition to Amnesty International's credible sources.

8 Mohseni-Eje'i does not specify what he means by drug offences but according to Article 8 of the Anti-Narcotics Law it could include anyone who "imports, manufactures, produces, distributes, exports, sends, deals in, puts on sale, keeps or stores, conceals or carries" more than 30 g of certain drugs or according to Article 4, more than 5 g of others. Articles 11, 12, 18, 26, and 35 list other offences such as "armed smuggling of drugs," "smuggling of drugs into prisons, barracks or rehabilitation centres," "hiring or supporting activities to commit crimes under the Anti-Narcotics Law," "being head of the gang or the network," "placing drugs in a locality in an attempt to accuse another person of a crime mentioned in the Anti-Narcotics Law," and "forcing children or mentally-ill persons to commit any crime mentioned in the Anti-Narcotics Law." The list of offences is not limited to the above.

9 سازمان تعزیرات حکومتی
10 سازمان قضایی نیروهای مسلح
11 E.g. Public and Revolutionary Courts/the State Discretionary Punishment Organization/the Judicial Organization of Armed Forces.

12 In the Persian language the direction of writing is from right to left.

References

1. Encyclopædia Iranica. *Ḥojjat-al-Eslām*. 2015. Available from: http://www.iranicaonline.org/articles/search/keywords:hojja.

2. Etebari M. *Iran press report: Fighting over sedition in the cabinet confirmations*. 2013. Available from: http://www.brookings.edu/blogs/markaz/posts/2013/08/15-iran-press-report-cabinet-confirmation-sedition.

3. Elliott MA. Universal Declaration of Human Rights. In: Ritzer G, editor. *Blackwell encyclopedias in social sciences: The Wiley-Blackwell encyclopedia of globalization*. Hoboken, NJ: Wiley; 2012.

4. UN. *International Covenant on Civil and Political Rights*. 1976. Available from: http://www.ohchr.org/en/professionalinterest/pages/ccpr.aspx.

5. UN Human Rights Committee. General Comment No. 6: Article 6 (Right to Life). Sixteenth Session (1982): United Nations; 1994. Contract No.: Doc. HRI/GEN/1/Rev.1. p. 177.

6. HRW. *Codifying repression: An assessment of Iran's new penal code*. New York: Human Rights Watch; 2012. p. 12.

7. Mouri L. *Gender segregation violates the rights of women in Iran*. International Campaign for Human Rights in Iran; 2014. Available from: http://www.iranhumanrights.org/2014/09/gender-segregation/.

8. UN. *The Universal Declaration of Human Rights.* United Nations General Assembly, editor: [Lake Success]; 1948.

9. IRI. *Constitution of the Islamic Republic of Iran.* Foundation for Iranian Studies; 1989. Available from: http://fis-iran.org/en/resources/legaldoc/constitutionislamic.

10. Sial O. *A guide to the legal system of the Islamic Republic of Iran.* New York University School of Law: Hauser Global Law School Program; 2006, Available from: http://www.nyulawglobal.org/globalex/Iran.htm-_The_Judiciary.

11. Lott DF, Sommer R. Seating arrangements and status. *Journal of Personality and Social Psychology.* 1967;7(1):90.

12. Abrahamian E. *A history of modern Iran.* New York: Cambridge University Press; 2008. p. 9.

13. Machin D, Mayr A. *How to do critical discourse analysis: A multimodal introduction.* London: SAGE; 2012. pp. 13, 67–69, 71, 78–79, 144, 153, 154, & 188.

14. Benyehuda N. The European witch craze of the 14th to 17th centuries—A sociologists perspective. *American Journal of Sociology.* 1980;86(1):2.

15. Amnesty International. Death sentences and executions: 2015. 2016. Contract No.: ACT 50/3487/2016. p. 49.

16. Amnesty International. *Iran's 'staggering' execution spree: Nearly 700 put to death in just over six months.* 2015. Available from: https://www.amnesty.org/en/latest/news/2015/07/irans-staggering-execution-spree/.

17. Shaheed A. *Report of the Secretary-General on the situation of human rights in the Islamic Republic of Iran.* United Nations; 2014, p. 18 [updated March 2014. Twenty-fifth session]. Available from: http://shaheedoniran.org/wp-content/uploads/2014/03/A-HRC-25-61-updated.pdf.

18. DPIC. *Executions and death sentences around the world.* Death Penalty Information Center; 2018. Available from: https://deathpenaltyinfo.org/death-penalty-international-perspective.

19. Hlinomaz O, Sheeran S, Bevilacqua C. *The death penalty for drug crimes in Iran: Analysis of Iran's international human rights obligations.* Essex: University of Essex; 2014. p. 12.

20. IHRDC. *English translation of the Islamic Republic of Iran's criminal code of procedure for public and revolutionary courts.* 2015. Available from: http://www.iranhrdc.org/english/human-rights-documents/iranian-codes/1000000026-english-translation-of-the-islamic-republic-of-irans-criminal-code-of-procedure-for-public-and-revolutionary-courts.html.

21. PressTV. *Ayatollah Khamenei pardons 1k+ prisoners.* 2014. Available from: http://www.presstv.com/detail/2014/10/11/381839/leader-grants-clemency-to-inmates/.

22. SDPO. *State Discretionary Punishment Organization (Official Website).* 2015. Available from: http://www.tazirat.gov.ir.

23. Mohammadi M. *Judicial reform and reorganization in 20th Century Iran: State-building, modernization and Islamicization.* New York & London: Routledge; 2008. p. 331.

24. JOAF. *Judicial Organization of Armed Forces (Official Website)*. 2015. Available from: http://www.imj.ir/Portal/Home/.
25. Rodley NS, Pollard M. *The treatment of prisoners under international law*. 3rd ed. Oxford: Oxford University Press; 2009. p. 315.
26. ICPS. *Prison population total*. 2014. Available from: http://www.prisonstudies.org/country/iran.
27. Mahdavi SH. "Worried"or "valiant"? The dialectic between Iran's nuclear negotiations and its domestic politics. Middle East Brief. 2014. p. 3.
28. SadraNewsAgency. *Gholam-Hossein Elham: Supreme Leader's keffiyeh in 97 has a specific meaning!*. 2014. Available from: http://sadranews.ir/index. php/اتزاه-ها ي-خ-ب ر/17603-غ-لامحس ی ن ا-لهما-چ فی ه-ادنخا ت ن-مقا م-ره ربی-رد-سا-ل-معناخی-داراد-خاص معناخی-داراد.html.
29. Machin D, Niblock S. Branding newspapers visual texts as social practice. *Journalism Studies*. 2008;9(2):254 & 255.
30. Mehta R, Zhu R. Blue or red? Exploring the effect of color on cognitive task performances. *Science*. 2009;323(5918):1226.
31. Asreelm. *Meaning and psychology of colors*. 2011. Available from: http://www.asreelm.com/meaning-of-colors/.
32. Moinipour S. UN treaty-based bodies and the Islamic Republic of Iran: Human rights dialogue (1990–2016). *Cogent Social Sciences*. 2018;4(1):1440910.

7 Iranian Migrants, IRIB, and Human Rights

Introduction

The empirical data presented thus far in this book reveal important elements on how international humanitarian and human rights principles are portrayed on the Iranian television. Television is a tool for delivering the ideology of the Iranian regime to the public.

It is, therefore, worth examining whether this attempt at ideological hegemony has had an impression on the Iranian people. This chapter assesses whether there is any correlation between what is portrayed in the news and the opinion of the recent Iranian migrants in relation to international human rights law. It explores the extent to which at least a percentage of the Iranian public, whence recent migrants come from, contributes to and participates in the dominant ideology and whether any counter-hegemony exists among the Iranian people. The chapter also seeks to find any similarities or contradictions between what the state television portrays as human rights issues and the opinions of recent migrants on such subjects. The migrants were studies to assess both their understanding of human rights issues portrayed on Iranian television and whether the group recognizes, accepts, or rejects the double standards that became evident in the analysis of Iranian news programs, discussed in Chapters 5 and 6.

Who Is Who?

General demographic data such as age,[1] gender, marital status, ethnicity, religion, educational attainment, and employment status of the recent immigrants while they still resided in Iran were collected for meaningful analysis and to understand the study population and its responses better.

Regarding gender, the participants turned out to be almost equally divided, with 51% of the respondents identifying as male and 50% as female. A small percentage of the men (5%) and women (3%) were 19–24 years of age; 16% of males and 15% of the females were from 25 to 34. Between the ages of 35 and 44, males comprised 6% and females 9%. Among those 45–54, 4% were males, and 8% were females. Finally, 19% of the men and 15% of women were 55 years of age and over.

With respect to participants' marital status, 57% were married, 30% were single, 7% were divorced, 2% were in a relationship, and 2% were widowed. An additional 2% of the participants did not respond to the question. The participants were from a range of religious backgrounds. As expected, the majority of the participants (54%) were Shi'a Muslims, 16% were Baha'is, 10% were Christians, and 1% was Zoroastrian. A full 16% of participants chose "Other" as a response to the religion question. In the box provided, participant responses varied from "None" to "No religion" to "No God"; 3% did not respond to the question.

Participants were also asked about their ethnicity. A large number of the participants (80%) indicated that they were Fars, which was expected, as they constitute Iran's majority ethnic group. Of the remaining participants, 6% were Azeri, 4% were Arab, 4% were Lur, and 3% were Kurd. One participant (1%), who identified as Gilaki,[2] chose "Other." Finally, 2% of the participants did not respond to the question.

Out of the total number of participants (101), 68% said they held a job when they were in Iran, and 32% said they did not. Jobs included hairdresser, teacher, butcher, clinical psychologist, journalist, lawyer, IT employee, commercial airline employee, oil company employee, cabinet maker, manager, clothing retail employee, engineer, municipality employee, chef, mechanic, student, construction employee, nurse, architect, medical doctor, lecturer, accountant, car representative, government employee, driver, factory employee, topographer, radiologist, and graphic designer.

With regard to educational attainment, 34% of the participants had graduated high school, and 15% had less than high school. Of the remaining participants, 9% had associate degrees[3] (1), 29% held a bachelor's degree, 8% held a master's degree, and 5% held a doctorate.

Who Consumes What?

Before asking any specific questions, the participants were asked what sources of news they used while they were living in Iran. As

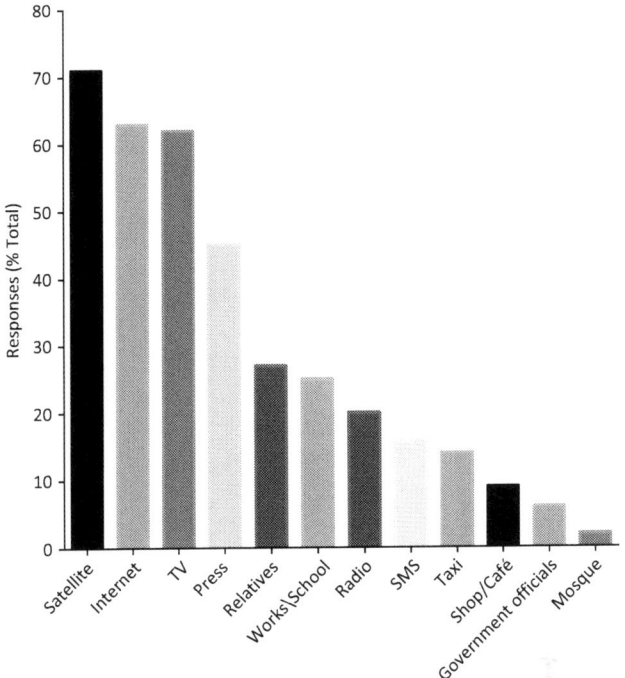

Figure 7.1 Sources of news information.

Figure 7.1 illustrates, state-run television was one of the top three sources of information, and 62% of the participants chose it as one of their choices of news source. 71% of the participants chose satellite television as one of their sources of information, and 63% chose the Internet. The press was the fourth choice, and 45% of the participants chose it as one of their sources of news information. Relatives (27%), work/school (25%), radio (20%), SMS (16%), taxi (14%), shop/café (9%), government officials (6%), and mosques (2%) were also choices for some participants.

The participants were then asked to choose only one of these choices as their "primary" source of news. For 37% of participants, the choice was satellite; 25% of the participants chose the Internet, and only 24% of the participants chose television as their primary source of news. The above is an interesting result for television and a significant drop from the result (62%) in the first question, but it is still consistent with the ranking. In order to make sure that the participants were knowledgeable enough about Islamic Republic of Iran Broadcasting (IRIB) to be able to continue with the questionnaire, they were then asked the following question: even if the Iranian state-run television was not one of your choices in question one, do you believe you are familiar with the news content of the television in Iran?

As mentioned earlier and illustrated in Figure 7.1, 62% of participants chose television as one of their sources of news. However, when asked about their familiarity with the IRIB content, 88% responded affirmatively. This result is significant because it shows that even though 38% of the respondents said they did not watch the news on the Iranian television, they were still familiar with its content and were exposed to it indirectly. It is possible, for example, that they watched the news on IRIB's official website www.irib.ir or other similar websites. Figure 7.2 illustrates the difference between participants' direct and indirect knowledge of TV news content in Iran. The bar on the left

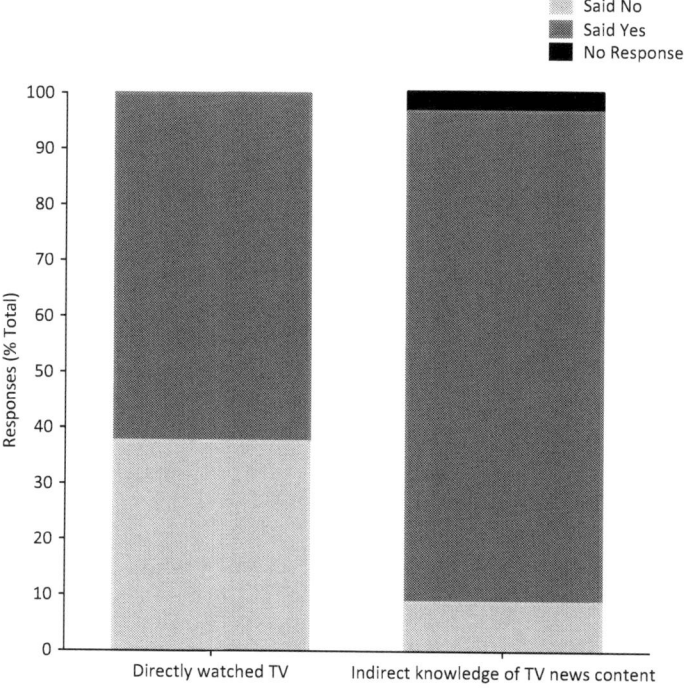

Figure 7.2 Comparison of direct versus indirect knowledge of TV news content in Iran.

shows the percentage of the participants who said they did not consume television as one of their sources of news information and those who said they used television as one of their sources of news information. The bar on the right shows the percentage of those who said they were not familiar with the news content of the Iranian television and those who said they were familiar with the news content of the Iranian television.

Who Knows What?

As noted earlier, 88% of the participants claimed that they were familiar with the content of state-run television, out of which 62% chose television as one of their sources of information, and 24% chose it as their primary source of information. Five statements were presented to the participants to delve deeper into their familiarity with IRIB news content. Table 7.1 marks the statements consecutively as S1, S2, S3, S4, and S5.[4] The relevant sources where they were extracted from are also included in the table. The participants were, of course, oblivious to the source of each statement and they had to guess, based on their familiarity with IRIB, whether the statements were likely to be broadcast on the Iranian television.

Table 7.1 Statements Presented to Survey Participants to Gauge Familiarity with State-Run News Language

	Statement	*Source*
S1	If our society really wanted to solve a problem we could. It would just require everybody saying that the issue "is important and significant."	Remarks by President Obama[a]
S2	The United Nations was born of the belief that the people of the world can live with their families in tranquility and resolve their differences peacefully. And yet we know that in too many parts of the world, this ideal has not been realized and is a mere dream.	Remarks by President Obama[b]
S3	To those who cling to power through corruption and deceit and the silencing of dissent, know that you are on the wrong side of history; but that we will extend a hand if you are willing to unclench your fist.	Remarks by President Obama[c]

(Continued)

Statement		Source
S4	If Shiite Muslims were getting killed in Iraq by ISIS instead of Yazidis, the United States would not have done anything to rescue them.	IRIB channel 1 news package 7 dated August 8, 2014
S5	The two favorite topics of the West are: minorities in Mosul and illegal sale of oil in Iraq and Syria by the terrorists.	IRIB channel 1 news package 7 dated August 8, 2014

The order presented here is not the same as the participants were presented with. The statements presented to participants were random. They have been organized here for statistical purposes.

[a] Remarks by President Obama and Prime Minister Abe of Japan in Joint Press Conference (April 28, 2015) available at: https://www.whitehouse.gov/the-press-office/2015/04/28/remarks-president-obama-and-prime-minister-abe-japan-joint-press-confere, Accessed on August 9, 2015.

[b] Obama's Speech to the United Nations General Assembly (September 23, 2009) available at: http://www.nytimes.com/2009/09/24/us/politics/24prexy.text.html?pagewanted=all&_r=0, Accessed on August 9, 2015.

[c] President Barack Obama's Inaugural Address (January 21, 2009) available at: https://www.whitehouse.gov/blog/inaugural-address, Accessed on August 9, 2015.

Figure 7.3A shows the general familiarity of the participants with the kind of language and themes used in IRIB news programs based on the statements they were presented with (Table 7.1). The general trend shows that more participants recognized that the statements made by Obama were unlikely to be broadcast from IRIB. With the two IRIB statements (S4 and S5), however, the participants were divided. Since the five-point Likert scale[5] gave the participants a range of options to choose from, a closer look at the data obtained from the responses was necessary.

In order to analyze the data, the middle choice of responses in the Likert scale—moderately unlikely—was taken to be neutral. The two extremes choices on the scale—(Not at all likely + Slightly likely) and (Very likely + Completely likely)—were combined to form two separate groups. Figure 7.3B illustrates the results, which shows that the majority of the participants recognized that it was unlikely for the statements made by Obama to be broadcast on IRIB. However, with the two statements that were broadcast on IRIB (S4 and S5), the results are not as straightforward and show no particular trend.

As Figure 7.3C illustrates, on average, 49% of the participants responded correctly to all statements, meaning that they recognized that the comments made by Obama were unlikely to be broadcast on the Iranian television, and they also realized that the statements made by IRIB were very likely to be broadcast on television. On the other hand,

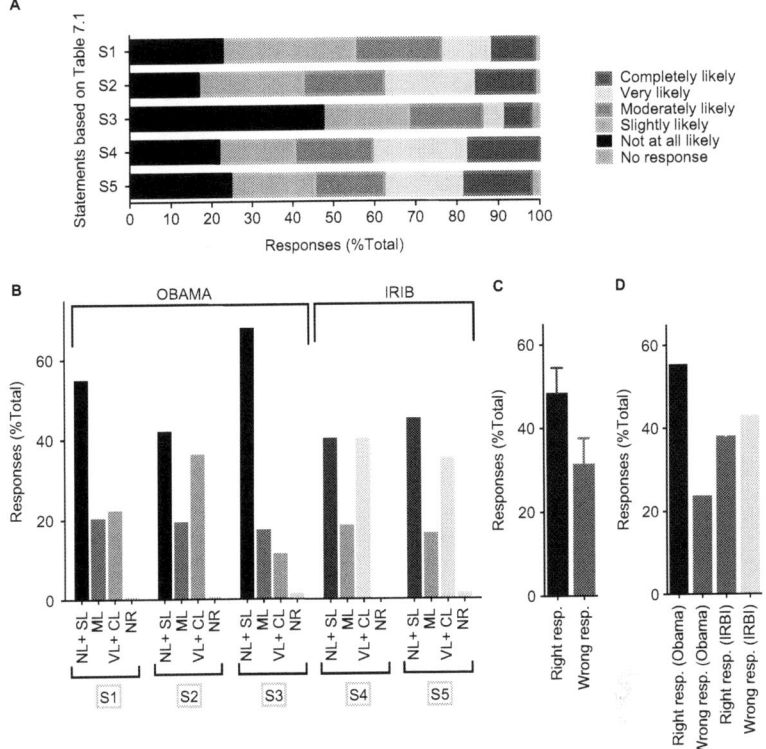

Figure 7.3 Likelihood of statements to be broadcast from IRIB. (A) The Likelihood of statements (S1, S2, S3, S4, and S5) from Table 7.1 to be broadcast from IRIB based on the opinion of the participants. (B) The opinion of the participants on the likelihood of the statements (S1–S5) from Table 7.1 (IRIB + Obama's statements) to be broadcast from the Iranian television. NL + SL stand for Not at all Likely + Slightly Likely, ML stands for Moderately Likely (taken to be neutral) and VL + CL stand for Very Likely + Completely Likely. NR stands for No Response for the participants who did not respond to these questions. (C) Total correct responses given by participants to all statements on the left and total incorrect responses given by participants to all statements on the right. For correct responses, the bars labeled (NL + SL) under S1, S2, and S3 plus the bars labeled (VL + CL) under S4 and S5 were combined. For incorrect responses, the data labeled (VL + CL) under S1, S2, and S3 were combined with data labeled (NL + SL) under S4 and S5 (D) Correct and incorrect responses given by participants based on the three statements by Obama on the left and correct and incorrect responses given by participants based on the two statements by IRIB on the right.

31% of the participants got all the statements wrong. That means that they did not recognize that Obama's comments were unlikely to be broadcast on television, and they failed to recognize that IRIB's statements were from Iranian television.

Breaking these results down even further, as illustrated in Figure 7.3D, 55% of the participants gave the correct response, meaning that they recognized the statements made by Obama were unlikely to be broadcast on the Iranian television. On the other hand, 24% of the participants were wrong in their choice—they did not recognize that Obama's statements were unlikely to be broadcast on Iranian television. These two results are significantly different and imply that more participants were certain about what was unlikely to be broadcast on Iranian television.[6] The participants who responded correctly to this question may have either been informed individuals or very familiar with the content of the Iranian television. Those who responded incorrectly to this question may have either been uninformed individuals or hesitant to say otherwise.

With regard to the responses given on IRIB statements (S4 and S5), the two bars on the right-hand side in Figure 7.3D suggest uncertainty and ambiguity. The percentage of those who responded correctly was 38%, and the percentage of those who answered incorrectly was 43%.[7] Since more participants got the responses wrong than right, a few conclusions can be deduced. First, the data presented in Figure 7.3D on IRIB statements suggest that vagueness and ambiguity in the language of IRIB may be responsible for the lack of recognition. Second, the participants who said they did not watch the news on the Iranian television at all and those who said they were not familiar with its content may have contributed to the increase in the number of participants who responded incorrectly to this question.

The ambiguity in the responses on IRIB statements could also point to how the participants viewed IRIB programming meaning that the participants who responded incorrectly may have watched IRIB but did not engage with it at any critical level. During the face-to-face interview, for example, one of the female participants stated that she solely watched the news on IRIB when she was in Iran, but everything that she watched was a lie. She was then asked how she knew the news was a lie and she responded, "Because others said so. Others said the news is wrong." The participants who answered correctly to this question may have been very familiar with the content and language used on Iranian television and could make the distinction easily. They may also have engaged with its content and compared and contrasted it with other news sources. During the face-to-face interviews, for example, one male participant stated that he knew that what IRIB showed on the news was all lies, but he still watched it because he was curious. He would then compare the IRIB content with that found on websites of foreign-based Persian television networks such as Manoto TV and BBC Persian by using Internet censorship circumvention.

In the questionnaire and the interview, the participants were also questioned about their knowledge of human rights. In general, the questions were based on either the human rights issues extracted from the news packages that were discussed in Chapters 5 and 6 or based on Iran's general human rights records and the dialogues between Iran and the United Nations' Committee, which is published separately in *Cogent Social Sciences* (2).

General Human Rights Knowledge

Participants were asked to give their opinion on two statements. The first statement said, "Qisas[8] (3) should be an integral principle of human rights," and the second statement read, "Every person enjoys equal rights in Iran." A high percentage of the participants disagreed with both statements. In other words, more people opposed Qisas than not, and more people realized inequality exists in Iran than not. Not everyone responded definitively to all these statements, however. Some participants, for example, chose a lower scale and made their responses dependent on the nature of the crime that resulted in Qisas.

With regard to the first statement, 68% of the participants disagreed, to varying degrees, that Qisas should be an integral principle of human rights. However, 20% agreed, to varying degrees, and 11% stayed neutral. During a face-to-face interview, one of the participants said that Qisas must be carried out for certain crimes such as rape. She also acknowledged that because the United Nations does not have enforcement power, Iran violates human rights in the name of cultural relativism.

In response to the second statement on equal rights for all, an overwhelming 85% of the participants recognized, to varying degrees, that people in Iran do not enjoy equal rights. During the face-to-face interview, one of the participants said, "The so-called human rights do not exist in Iran." However, even with the continuous exposure of human rights violations in Iran, 10% of the participants thought that all Iranians enjoy equal rights; 4% of the participants were neutral on the topic.

The participants were asked whether Muslims, Christians, Jews, and Baha'is in Iran all enjoy equal human rights. To varying degrees,

20% of the participants believed these groups enjoy equal rights, and, to varying degrees, 72% disagreed, saying that members of these religions do not have equal human rights. The latter result is a 13% drop from the 85% of participants who recognized that people in Iran do not enjoy equal rights, but it is still a high percentage. Except for individuals belonging to a few categories such as the 19–24 age group and the associate and master's degrees, a small percentage of the participants in every other category completely agreed that Muslims, Christians, Jews, and Baha'is enjoy the same human rights in Iran. While the majority of the participants were aware that religious groups in Iran do not have equal rights as Shi'a Muslims, there was a small percentage of the participants who thought otherwise. Even some of the highly educated seemed unaware of human rights violations against religious minorities in Iran. The inability to take cognizance of the palpable inequality that exists in the country could be due to the fact that the media in Iran, whose function is to raise awareness, has failed so to do. In addition, since the lack of awareness exists even among some religious minorities, this could mean that these participants' knowledge of human rights is generally poor.

Knowledge of Human Rights in Relation to the Media

Participants were also asked a few human rights-related questions especially in connection with the media. They were asked, for example, how important it was for state news to cover human rights-related issues in Iran. This question was asked to determine whether the participants were aware of the individual right to freedom of speech, which according to the stipulations of Article 19 of the Universal Declaration of Human Rights comprises of "three complementary rights: the right to hold opinions, the right to seek and receive information and last but not least the freedom to impart one's own views and ideas" (4). The human rights questions related to the media were mostly focused on the right to seek and receive information even though freedom of speech, as Kulesza states, "is not an absolute right" hence restrictions of "certain content does not deem the infraction illegal" (4). In any case, Article 19, paragraph 2 of the International Covenant on Civil and Political Rights obliges states to guarantee such freedom even though paragraph 3 of the same article restricts this obligation to law and necessity.

For 27% of the participants, to varying degrees, it was not that important for IRIB to cover news on human rights. For these participants, either human rights-related incidents and issues did not matter, or they thought of television solely as a medium for entertainment. At the other extreme, however, again to varying degrees, 64% of the participants felt it was important for IRIB to cover human rights issues and related matters. To determine how precisely the participants understood the word "human" in the phrase "human rights," they were asked about Afghan refugees in Iran, a marginalized group of immigrants who are mistreated in various ways by both the government and the public (5). The participants were asked how appropriate it is for the human rights issues as they relate to the Afghan refugees to be covered in Iran's state news. The results were then compared with the results of similar questions on human rights-related issues of the Americans and on human rights-related issues in general. The complete results of this comparison have been published in *The International Journal of Human Rights* in an article entitled "Refugees against refugees: The Iranian migrants' perception of the human rights of Afghans in Iran" (6). The results are briefly discussed here again due to their particular importance.

Based on the responses, the majority of the participants (64%) were positive about the coverage of general human rights issues in IRIB news. Almost the same percentage of the participants (60%) also believed that the human rights-related issues of Americans should be covered in the news. There was a drastic change in attitude, however, once the participants were asked about the human rights-related issues of Afghans. The number of positive responses dropped to 25%, which means that the majority of the participants did not want the human rights-related issues of Afghans covered in the news. This open discrimination also came from those who are themselves considered persecuted minorities in Iran, which leads one to conclude that the word "human," as is meant in the international human rights law, is not fully understood as an all-inclusive concept. The face-to-face interviews also supported that participants were confident about the use of the word human rights but lacked the knowledge about its principles and had a general discriminatory approach toward them.

A separate question allowed for the analysis of data on whether the prejudice against Afghans extended to other minority groups. Participants were asked whether the human rights issues of religious minorities should be covered on IRIB news. A full 80% of the participants agreed that IRIB news should cover human rights issues related to religious minorities; 12% disagreed. This 80% is higher than the percentage of those (64%) who initially said human rights issues, in general, must be covered on the news. Within religious minority groups themselves, a small percentage did not feel that human rights issues of religious minorities should be covered on IRIB news. Such a response may suggest that the participants were familiar with certain human rights terms but were not exactly knowledgable about what they entail.

Recognition and Understanding of News Content

As indicated previously, a partial aim of the research was to elucidate whether there is any correlation between what Iranian state television portrays on human rights and what recent Iranian migrants think of such portrayals. The aim was also to establish whether the participants recognize, accept, or reject human rights as portrayed on the news. The following subsection will discuss the results based on the responses that contradicted and corresponded with what is shown on IRIB. The subsequent subsection will analyze the data to determine the participants' recognition, acceptance, or rejection of what is portrayed on IRIB news programs.

Correlations: Recent Immigrants' Opinions versus IRIB News

Analysis of the news content on television in Chapters 5 and 6 revealed that IRIB manipulated human rights-related news about certain events. Simultaneously, IRIB suppressed some news content and obscured others for political reasons. To determine whether their opinions reflected what is shown on television, participants were asked whether they agreed or disagreed with the following two statements as broadcast on the news: "Miscreant individuals must be executed," and "The Supreme Leader of Iran is an advocate of human rights because he gives amnesty to and reduces punishment of prisoners every year on Eid-e Fetr."

With regard to the first statement, 22% of the participants agreed, to varying degrees, that the miscreants should be executed while 15% preferred to stay neutral. Out of the 22% of the participants who agreed, 10% were 55 years old and over. The next age group with the highest percentage of agreements (7%) was between 25 and 34 years of age. Gender-wise, 10% of the participants who agreed to this statement were men, and 12% were women. Out of the total of 22%, 16% were married, and 5% were single.

The responses were also analyzed based on religion. Out of the total percentage of those who agreed with the statement about executing miscreants, 14% were Shi'a, 3% were Christian, and 3% marked "Other," which included those who believed in "no God" and "no religion." Ethnically, 18% of the participants were Fars, and 3% were

Azeri. Based on the data, there seems to be no correlation between education and the participants' opinion on execution.

When it came to the second statement, 13% of the participants agreed, to varying degrees, that the Supreme Leader's clemency during Eid-e Fetr demonstrates that he is a human rights advocate, while 10% of the participants were neutral. Out of the total 13% of the participants, 8% were 55 and over and 4% were between 25 and 34 years of age. Out of the total who agreed with this statement, 7% were men, and 6% were women; 8% were married, and 4% were single.

The data was also analyzed based on religious affiliation. Of the participants who agreed that Khamenei is a human rights advocate, 10% were Shi'a, 2% were Baha'i, and 1% was Christian. Ethnically, 9% were Fars, 2% were Azeri, and 1% was Lur. No one with the two highest educational levels—master's or doctorate—agreed with this statement.

The percentage of the positive responses to the two statements, which correspond to what is portrayed on television, is small compared to the percentage of those who answered negatively to them. In response to the statement that miscreants should be executed 62% disagreed. Even though this percentage is the sum of varying degrees of disagreements, it is still the majority. The highest percentage of those who disagreed (20%) fell in the age group 25–34. There was not much of a difference in responses based on gender. To varying degrees, 31% of men and 32% of women felt that miscreants should not be executed. 22% of the respondents who disagreed with this statement were single, and 34% were married.

The educational background of the participants whose responses contradicted that of television portrayal was distributed throughout all educational levels. Ethnically, 50% of the participants were Fars. The rest were, in smaller proportions, Azeri (3%), Kurd (2%), Arab (4%), and Lur (3%). In terms of religion, 29% of the respondents were Shi'a, 6% were Christian, 1% was Zoroastrian, 12% were Baha'i, and 13% indicated they belonged to the "Other" category, which constituted mostly those who either did not have a religion or did not believe in God.

When it came to the second statement regarding the Supreme Leader being a human rights advocate, the percentage of the participants who disagreed was also overwhelmingly high—77% of the participants disagreed, to varying degrees, that the Supreme Leader's clemency during Eid-e Fetr had any relation with an act of advocacy for human rights. The disagreement with the statement among the group between 25 and 34 was particularly high (25%). It also did not matter whether the participants identified with a particular religion. The same was true of ethnicity—61% of the participants were Fars, but participants from other ethnic backgrounds also disagreed with this statement. There was no particular trend in educational attainment either. A percentage of the participants from all educational backgrounds disagreed with this statement. Simply put, the majority of participants disagreed that miscreants should be executed even though a fair percentage qualified their responses depending on who exactly is a miscreant. The majority of participants also did not agree that the Supreme Leader is a human rights advocate, despite IRIB's positive portrayal of him.

Acceptances and Rejections

Television is a non-coercive cultural tool used by the Iranian regime to deliver its Islamic ideology. However, wherever hegemonic power exists, there is reciprocity between both the dominant and the dominated. In other words, according to Nicola Pratt, "It is not merely the case that one class/group exercise power at the expense of another. The 'dominated' also contribute to and participate in their domination through their actions, which are informed through their worldview" (7). The extent to which IRIB news consumption played a role in the participants' lives was also examined. The data were analyzed to see whether the participants recognized the dichotomy that exists on IRIB and whether they accept or reject it.

Participants were asked whether they agreed or disagreed with the following statement: "The United States discriminates against black people." In response, 43% of the participants disagreed, to varying degrees, that the United States discriminates against black people. While 34% of the participants agreed with this statement, 23% neither agreed nor disagreed.

The information regarding discrimination in the United States, most likely, could only reach to the participants through Iranian state media since all were recent immigrants from Iran. Therefore, the agreement among 34% of participants that the United States discriminates against black people has possibly been picked up either from what was reported on Iranian television, the Internet, or satellite, bearing in mind that Internet and satellite censorship are on-going in Iran.

During a face-to-face interview, one participant felt that the coverage of foreign events on Iranian television was "somewhat positive." She stated:

> They showed what was in their gain and favor of the government policy. What they showed was perhaps a true reflection of what happened abroad. I mean it was completely real. However, it is

also quite possible that they also cut some things, which made it difficult to trust the news they were reflecting in Iran too much. I mean I always watched the Iranian television with suspicion.

This participant's statement suggests some internal conflict. She starts by reacting positively to the idea that IRIB's coverage of foreign news events is real. Then, she casts doubt on this idea and takes a more skeptical stance. This conflict shows a dichotomy in the thinking process of the participants, which mirrors the dichotomy apparent in the Iranian regime's portrayal of human rights even though most participants were quite open about their resentment toward the regime. Another person thought everything IRIB covered about events in foreign countries was unreal except for trivial news such as the weather reports.

Another participant believed that IRIB only airs and magnifies the negative human rights-related issues of foreign countries. This participant also thought that IRIB's emphasis on the negative affairs of the West blows them out of proportion. In addition, broadcasting them over and over again is a tactic to convince Iranians that Iran is the safest and the best place to live. The participant maintained that the regime does not want to show the higher living standards of the Western countries and their relative respect for human rights so that the Iranian people remain aloof and oblivious to their rights. In other words, keeping people ignorant and content with their current situation leads to fewer demands on the state and thus allows the regime to exercise more control. Another participant believed that the events in foreign countries are portrayed on IRIB in such a way to show that life in other countries is miserable and the Iranian regime is doing the people a favor by creating great living conditions in Iran compared to everywhere else.

Going back to the responses of the participants on discrimination in the United States, such acquired knowledge on the part of the participants could also be attributed to the participants being immigrants. Immigration is perhaps one of the key elements that set this group apart from those still living in Iran. Immigrants may have more interest in following the news of foreign countries, hence more knowledgeable about it. During a face-to-face interview, for example, one participant said that he always followed the foreign news when he was in Iran. He was interested in knowing what was going on because he always intended to leave Iran. Another participant said that she started following the foreign news as soon as the family started thinking about leaving Iran.

While this heightened interest in following foreign news by those planning to leave Iran may explain why 34% of the participants recognized that discrimination against black people is an issue in the United States, it is surprising that 43% of the participants disagreed with this statement. Many participants accused IRIB of disseminating false information about foreign countries—30% of participants rated the coverage of human rights issues of foreign countries by IRIB "very poor," and 29% rated it "poor." Disagreement with the statement that the United States discriminates against black people might be because of participants' distrust of the Iranian regime and IRIB. Thus, if IRIB portrays the United States as discriminating against black people, then skeptics reject it by default and conclude that the United States does not discriminate against black people.

In addition, 23% of the participants stayed neutral on the question. This percentage is a relatively high number. Participants may have been genuinely uninformed or preferred to stay neutral for fear of getting involved in what they may think are political issues. Even though in essence discrimination against black people is a human rights issue, it became apparent that the Islamic Republic of Iran has successfully made politics and human rights inseparable in the minds of the public, especially on issues related to the United States and Israel. One participant, for example, became anxious as soon as she saw a question involving Israel and the United States asking whether their citizens should have the same fundamental rights saying, "This is too political, so I cannot answer it."

The high percentage of neutral responses raises another question: do participants recognize that human rights issues are being addressed on IRIB? During a face-to-face interview, one participant categorically rejected the idea that IRIB news covers *any* human rights issues. In addition, all participants were asked whether they thought it probable for IRIB to cover foreign human rights issues? A full 54% thought it was not probable, and only 18% thought it was probable. Participants seemed more certain about IRIB's coverage of domestic issues—73%, to varying degrees, thought it was not probable that IRIB would cover domestic human rights issues. Only 9%, also to varying degrees, thought it was probable.

The data show that for a large number of participants, the mere association of human rights with the regime apparatus, i.e. IRIB was non-correlational, more so when the human rights issues were associated with Iranians living in Iran. The fact that 18% of the participants saw it probable that IRIB would cover foreign human rights issues whereas only 9% of the participants saw it probable that IRIB would cover domestic human rights issues could go back to the analysis of

IRIB news programs. The analysis showed that the human rights language was transparent when it came to the coverage of foreign human rights issues but became very vague and ambiguous when it came to the coverage of domestic human rights issues.

That many participants did not think it probable for domestic and foreign human rights issues to be covered on IRIB news may be because many participants did not seem to understand what human rights issues are in the first place. In response to one question, where participants were asked to rate the coverage of domestic human rights issues by the state-run Iranian news media, 46% said the coverage was "very poor," and 25% said it was "poor." Only 2% rated it "good," and 1% rated it "excellent." Once again, 27% stayed neutral, perhaps due to the fear of criticizing the regime.

Participants were asked more specific questions based on the analysis of IRIB news in order to delve deeper into and deduce whether there are any further correlations between human rights portrayal on IRIB news and the immigrants' opinion on such portrayals. In one of the analyzed news packages, Palestinians were depicted as innocent with their rights being violated while Israelis were shown as evil people who must be stripped off their rights. When participants were asked if they felt that Palestinians and Israelis should have the same human rights, 86% of the participants agreed, to varying degrees, that Palestinians and Israelis should have the same human rights. In other words, 86% of the participants rejected what was shown on IRIB. Only 6% of the participants disagreed and felt that Israelis and Palestinians should not have the same human rights, hence accepting IRIB's message.

Participants were asked a similar question about a few additional countries. This time they were asked whether the human rights of Iranians, Afghans, Palestinians, Israelis, and Americans should be the same. Once again, an overwhelming percentage of the participants (91%) agreed that they should. This result is surprising since in an earlier question a large number of participants seemed to have reservations against Afghans.

This discrepancy may have two explanations. One explanation could be that the participants took Afghans to mean Afghans living in Afghanistan in the earlier question and not Afghan refugees living in Iran, who are, due to Iran's own growing unemployment issue, accused of "stealing jobs by underbidding and are seen as unfair recipients of the limited social services and resources" (8). This explanation compares with the results obtained from the responses to the question, which asked the opinion of the participants on whether human rights should mean the same thing in Iran, the United States, Gaza, and Afghanistan. Again, 86% of the participants agreed, to varying degrees, that human rights should have the same meaning in all the countries mentioned earlier including in Afghanistan.

Another explanation could be that Afghanistan was grouped with other countries and nationalities, and it is possible that responses were based on generalities. In any case, the 91% of the participants who agreed with the statement that Iranians, Afghans, Palestinians, Israelis, and Americans should have the same human rights rejected what was shown on IRIB television. Only 3% of the participants disagreed with this question and seemed to accept IRIB's portrayal that individuals deserve different rights based on their nationalities, religions, and ethnicities.

Conclusion

Even though satellite and the Internet were the first and second choice of news sources for most participants, the majority claimed that they were familiar with IRIB news content. For most participants, however, there was skepticism over what IRIB shows as opposed to what is unlikely to be shown.

In general, most participants were resentful toward IRIB and distrusted the news. The lack of correlation between their responses and the human rights-related issues portrayed on the news, however, does not mean that the participants were necessarily familiar with human rights principles or universal values.

The results do not show a clear demographic pattern. No particular group, gender, ethnic group, religious group, age group, or educational level stood out for any particular question. That no one specific trend could be elicited shows the diversity of the population under study and the porous nature of the environment in Iran. The absence of a trend may be due to the hybrid nature of the regime, which functions under contemporary authoritarianism. It may also go back to the invented tradition and the re-traditionalism that Khomeini introduced, which bear inherent flaws that do not allow for an entirely sealed *ummat*.

The results, however, show an evident resistance on the part of the majority of the participants. The resistance to believing what is shown on IRIB, the lack of trust, and a general resentment toward it are counter-hegemony measures assumed by the majority of the participants, perhaps due to the power created through the "hegemonic, official Islamic culture." Unfortunately, resentment toward the regime and its apparatuses, which have violated the human rights of many over the years, does not contribute to the better understanding of international human rights law and its principles. That the Iranian regime uses human rights for propaganda purposes and withholds information on human rights principles from public dissemination are gross violations of the regime's obligation to promote and its ultimate failure to educate the public on human rights.

Notes

1 For ethical reasons individuals under 18 years of age were not included in the study.
2 Gilani or Gilak: native to province of Gilan in the North of Iran.
3 An associate degree in Iran is equivalent to a college degree.
4 For analysis purposes, the order of the statements was intentionally changed from that which the participants were presented within the questionnaire.
5 The five-point Likert scale for this question contained: completely likely, very likely, moderately likely, slightly likely, and not at all likely.
6 An unpaired two-tailed t-test was carried out to determine the significant of this difference. The p-value obtained was 0.0373, which is significantly less than 0.05 with a p-value summary of (*). Hence, statistically the mean value of those who responded correctly to Obama's statements was significantly different than those who responded incorrectly.
7 The statistical significance of this result could not be determined since there were only two data points ($n = 2$) per group included in this comparison, i.e. S4 and S5. The trends of responses were not immediately obvious from the pilot that was done on five samples prior to the full launch of the study. Otherwise, more statements from IRIB could have been included in the questionnaire to determine statistical significance.
8 Qisas is an Islamic criminal jurisprudence law which allows the victims of the crimes to demand "retaliation in kind: an eye for an eye, a life for a life."

References

1. Soleimanpour H, Gholipouri C, Salarilak S, Raoufi P, Vahidi RG, Rouhi AJ, et al. Emergency department patient satisfaction survey in Imam Reza Hospital, Tabriz, Iran. *International Journal of Emergency Medicine.* 2011;4(2):3.
2. Moinipour S. UN treaty-based bodies and the Islamic Republic of Iran: Human rights dialogue (1990–2016). *Cogent Social Sciences.* 2018;4(1):1–27.
3. Hascall SC. Restorative justice in Islam: Should Qisas be considered a form of restorative justice? *Berkeley Journal of Middle Eastern & Islamic Law.* 2012;4(1):35–78.
4. Kulesza J. Social media censorship vs. state responsibility for human rights violations: Case study of the Arab Spring Uprising in Egypt. In: Pătruţ M, Pătruţ B, editors. *Social media in politics: Case studies on the political power of social media.* Public Administration and Information Technology. 13. Cham: Springer; 2014:260-261.

5. Small Media. *National fabric: Iran's ethnic minorities.* 2015, p. 5. Available from: http://smallmedia.org.uk/nationalfabric/Nationalfabric.pdf.
6. Moinipour S. Refugees against refugees: The Iranian migrants' perception of the human rights of Afghans in Iran. *The International Journal of Human Rights.* 2017;21(7):823–37.
7. Pratt N. Bringing politics back in: Examining the link between globalization and democratization. *Review of International Political Economy.* 2004;11(2):318.
8. Bhatnagar A. *Iran: Understanding the policy towards Afghan refugees.* IPCS: Institute of Peace and Conflict Studies; 2012. Available from: http://www.ipcs.org/article/Afg-Iran/iran-understanding-the-policy-towards-afghan-refugees-3683.html.

8 Human Rights Promotion: An Unmet Obligation

The Trodden Path: Dichotomy in Khomeini's Ideology

Although many theories and concepts assist with the understanding of the results of this research, a few concepts need to be revisited to explain what has changed in Iran since the time of Khomeini. This change may be subtle and to the dismay of the Islamic Republic of Iran, since one of the slogans of the Iranian regime and its supporters has always been "following Imam Khomeini's path." In January 2016, the Iranian President, Hassan Rouhani, "urged all Iranians to follow the path of the Founder of the Islamic Revolution saying his right path would not be forgotten" (1). The results of this research demonstrate that Iranian nationalism has not been rejected and has not been replaced by the pan-Islamic concept of *ummat*. Khomeini's vision of *ummat* was the establishment of a united global Ummah and the universalization of Islamic sovereignty, as a strategy upon which international peace and security could be permanently built (2). This ideology has not been fully realized and a dichotomy of nationalism and *ummat* has been manifested in the regime's vision of an imagined community.

IRIB, Human Rights, and Democratization

A dichotomy is apparent not only in the regime's vision of *ummat* as an imagined community but also in almost everything associated with the regime. This dichotomy exists due to the hybrid nature of the political system in Iran, which is perhaps responsible for the proliferation of the never-ending "contradictory institutions, units and policies, in addition to individual and institutional differences and interests" (3). As one of these institutions, Islamic Republic of Iran Broadcasting (IRIB) has become one of the most extensive and richest cultural units that reports directly to the Supreme Leader of the Islamic Republic and has received more than $329,337,373 (United States) from the government, placing it at the top of the list of the recipients of the government's cultural budget (4).

Since the beginning of the revolution, the Iranian regime has tried to bring back a so-called tradition that did not exist at the time of Prophet Muhammad. Therefore, the Islamicization of a modern means of communication is dichotomous at its very core. The Iranian regime firmly believes that the role that media plays in the transformation of Iran is pivotal in all areas of development, including political, economic, social, and cultural areas (5).

Taking culture as one example, how is development meant to take place if the radio and television, as cultural tools, are monopolized with no public right of access? Even if the hybrid nature of Iran allows for some democratic impulses, rentierism in Iran, which "resists socio-political demands and pressure from below, strongly discourage[s] democratization" (6). Like any other dichotomous and ambiguous expressions of hybridity resulting from the re-traditionalization of Islam, there are many dichotomies and ambiguities due to the regime's attempt to "reconcile 'Islam' with 'democracy' and human rights," even though such reconciliation has been painful for the Islamic Republic (3). This attempt is apparent in the regime's dialogue, if not in action, with the United Nations (UN) and the adoption of human rights language over the years (7). Whatever the reason, the Iranian regime has committed itself to the UN and five core treaties.

Human Rights Portrayal on the Iranian News

The Shah's secularization and modernization efforts brought about certain dependencies on the West and Khomeini tried to eliminate them. Those who questioned the Shah's modernization efforts believed that "Westernization was merely a new disguise for political dominance and cultural imperialism, a threat to Iranian and Islamic culture" (8). This thought process became Khomeini's best weapon for creating an antagonistic environment toward the West and labeling the West as "them" and the *ummat* as "us."

In addition, the transition between the two political systems—from an autocratic monarchy to a contemporary form of hybrid authoritarianism—left Iran with various forms of ambiguous and dichotomous expressions. Hybridity is a natural outcome of a revolution; yet the expressions of hybridity are accentuated with intentional political motives. The Islamic Republic of Iran set in motion a complicated political system that resulted in ambiguous and dichotomous laws and regulations. The dichotomies and ambiguities have also found their way into state-run television. By delving deeper into such manifestations, it has become clear that the expressions of hybridity also exist in the way human rights are portrayed in the Iranian media. While human rights language is clear in the reportage of foreign events, it is ambiguous in media coverage of domestic affairs. Therefore, there is a dichotomy in how the principles of international human rights law are disseminated.

This book has illustrated that the principles of international human rights and humanitarian laws have become tools for the Iranian regime to continue with its antagonization efforts. The creation of an antagonistic environment gives the Iranian regime power and legitimacy. IRIB news is commissioned to portray certain issues as violations of human rights in the West, especially in the United States and Israel. Khomeini branded these two countries as the "enemies of Islam" in 1979. While some of these issues might be violations of human rights, they are generalized, manipulated, and used for propaganda purposes.

Meanwhile, out of all the Islamic countries that are meant to be part of the pan-Islamic ideology, only Palestine has found its way into the state and IRIB policies as a permanently oppressed victim that needs the support of the Islamic Republic of Iran and which the regime has been faithfully concerned about on air over the years. As early as 1979, Khomeini had "asked his nation to mark Friday as a day of solidarity with the Palestinian people" (9). It is, therefore, worth reiterating the law that obliges the Radio and Television Organization and the Ministry of Culture and Islamic Guidance to address this issue. The law requires these entities

> to mobilize their forces and to cooperate with independent media worldwide and the media in the Islamic World, to communicate the oppression of the Palestinian people, especially those oppressed individuals residing in the Gaza strip, and the violent crimes of the Zionist regime, which are against human rights, to the rest of the world (10).

During the face-to-face interviews, it was apparent to some participants that the Iranian regime tries to show the West as the worst place to live and Iran as a place that bestows to its people all that is necessary for a pure Islamic life. IRIB uses human rights language to make sure this message is understood. However, to portray such an image,

IRIB uses information selectively, taking information out of context manipulating images, and mistranslating quoted material. The manipulation of the news is multifaceted. The news is manipulated, and a particular message is conveyed through the structuring of sentences, use of leading voice tones, and body language.

The victims of human rights violations, as determined by IRIB, are presented in intentional agonizing, harrowing, and distressing terms with the use of heartrending music, images, and footage. The very long coverage time and news placement of certain victims outweigh the coverage time and placement of other human rights victims. The dichotomy lies in whom the Iranian regime considers victims of human rights violations and how the international human rights principles are used in foreign versus domestic news coverage.

Across Time: From Khomeini's Ideology to IRIB News

Khomeini won the hearts and minds of the nation in 1979 with his promise of an independent community cleansed from Westoxication. He created an imagined community with an alternative collective religio-cultural identity based on Shi'a moral values. The suppression of human rights language and the lack of reporting on human rights violations within Iran seem to be a way to prove that Khomeini's promise has been fulfilled. The minimal mention of any human rights-related issue such as executions comes with a completely justified explanation in very general and ambiguous terms. The viewer is always kept aloof from the identities of these victims or "miscreants," the nature of their crimes, and whether they had the right to fair trials and due processes. The highest judicial authority, appointed by the Supreme Leader, requests Iranians to protect themselves against these "miscreants." At the opposite end of the spectrum, IRIB has also become known for broadcasting forced confessions in show trials (11), another method justifying human rights violations.

Khomeini's re-traditionalism has created an antagonistic environment in which those who do not conform to his imagined collective religio-cultural identity are labeled as Westoxicated and antagonistic. This "othering" is the ideological hegemony imposed through IRIB as a cultural tool. Interestingly, in domestic coverage of human rights issues, the victims of human rights violations are not the focus. The Supreme Leader and the regime apparatuses are! In line with the notion that Iran is the best place in the world to live, the Supreme Leader and the regime are portrayed as merciful entities in a mental "wheeling and dealing" contract with the people of Iran. The people of Iran need to conform to the collective religio-cultural identity based on Shari'a law in exchange for benefits, protection, right to life and freedom. Those who violate this contract lose their human rights.

Migrants: Human Rights Perception and IRIB

The Islamic Republic of Iran's human rights record started poorly in 1979, which has become even darker over the years. The results of this research show that at least the majority of those who have left Iran believe that the Iranian regime is oppressive. For example, 72% of the participants realized that Muslims, Christians, Jews, and Baha'is do not enjoy equal rights in Iran. However, participants seem to lack the knowledge and the awareness of what constitute human rights principles. If the Iranian regime fulfilled its obligation to promote international human rights principles, then who would give it legitimacy? It seems, therefore, to be for the best interest of the Iranian regime to keep the public ignorant of universal values.

The Iranian people give legitimacy to the regime with their "public opinion" informed and shaped by the state-owned and state-controlled media. In return, they get a "good" life in Iran, as framed by the regime. They also keep quiet about human rights violations since they do not necessarily know when and what rights are being violated.

The results, however, suggest an evident resistance on the part of the majority of the participants. The resistance created as a result of the regime's ideological hegemony through the culture of broadcasting represents itself as a cultural counter-hegemony by the participants. It seems that the majority of participants say and believe the opposite of what is shown on IRIB even though they lack the knowledge or understanding of human rights principles. The Iranian regime, however, seems to have succeeded in keeping its position, at least against a fair percentage of the population that gives it legitimacy, by suppressing domestic human rights information in media and misusing it in foreign news coverage. Despite resistance against the regime and its apparatuses, the Iranian regime has maintained its stability.

The fact that the regime has sustained itself all these years may also go back to the 1979 Revolution. The success of a revolution and its smooth transition toward democracy are rare. This transition depends on the state, its strength, and its aptitude in dominating and controlling the public using sustained coercive measures (12). If the state is consistent and successful in its coercion, then it can crush dissent and enjoy "significant illegitimacy." It can also repress any widespread feeling of "relative deprivation" in society (12).

With the majority of study participants, all of whom migrated out of Iran for various reasons, their position seems to have shifted, and through resistance, they seem to be on the winning side. However, the idea that a shift in position is enough to bring about structural changes and invade the ideological complex that supports the ruling system (13) does not seem to be sufficient even if, theoretically, the resistance also exists in the majority of Iranians living in Iran. Education and raising awareness on human rights principles and issues are also important because, as the results show, the lack of human rights knowledge means that individuals go back to the same ideological ideas they have been exposed to for years on end.

There are a general dislike and distrust toward the IRIB news, but there is an underlying and unconscious mark of the regime's efforts to safeguard the collective religio-cultural identity. That even some of those minority groups persecuted in Iran thought Khamenei to be a human rights advocate or that "miscreants" should be executed may either suggest fear to say otherwise or present a correlation between what is shown on television and what the Iranian public thinks about the portrayal. It must be noted, however, that associations do not necessarily "establish causality" (14).

The acrimonious feeling of most participants toward IRIB does not change the fact that the majority still consumed it. A full 62% of the participants chose television as one of their sources of news in Iran, and 88% said they are familiar with its content. The lack of promotion and awareness of human rights principles makes media yet another tool for human rights violation since the "[w]idespread information about human rights comes mostly from the mass media. If the media fails to report fairly, accurately, or consistently, public perceptions will be unfair, inaccurate or inconsistent" (15). Raising awareness, informing and educating the public on even the most basic cultural habits and traditions that feed into cycles of self-suppression and self-annihilation, such as following sources of imitation who think and decide for their followers, might be the only transformative avenue toward a sustainable democracy. This issue was apparent during the administration of surveys, as a few participants struggled with thinking on their own.

Media, just like any other powerful technology, can be constructive or destructive. The empirical results indicate that Iran is not constructively using the media. The standards defining the human rights responsibilities of media professionals and the state are already embedded in human rights instruments. Article 19 of UDHR, for example, states, "Everyone has the right to freedom of opinion and expression;

this right includes freedom to hold opinions without interference and to seek, receive and impart information and ideas through any media and regardless of frontiers." Article 19 of the International Covenant on Civil and Political Rights (ICCPR) states

1   Everyone shall have the right to hold opinions without interference.
2   Everyone shall have the right to freedom of expression; this right shall include freedom to seek, receive and impart information and ideas of all kinds, regardless of frontiers, either orally, in writing or in print, in the form of art, or through any other media of his choice.
3   The exercise of the rights provided for in paragraph 2 of this article carries with it special duties and responsibilities. It may therefore be subject to certain restrictions, but these shall only be such as are provided by law and are necessary:

    a   For respect of the rights or reputations of others;
    b   For the protection of national security or of public order (ordre public), or of public health or morals.

Article 13 of the Convention on the Rights of the Child also reiterates the earlier point with regard to the rights of the child. These are just a few examples, but considering the results discussed in this book, it seems essential to put more emphasis on educating, training, and promoting the human rights responsibilities of media professionals and those in power. This focus could be the basis of the media crafting its response through ethical codes.

Iran's discriminatory policies and the dissemination of information to incite hatred and defame internal and external antagonists have resulted in inactivity on the part of the Iranian citizens to the extent that the Supreme Leader has had to use the culture of "wheeling and dealing" on many occasions. One instance was when Iran was preparing itself for legislative elections on February 26, 2016.[1] In a speech, as reported by Gooya News (dated January 20, 2016), Ali Khamenei made a social contract between the state and the people. He asked all members of the society to honor the state and to give it power and legitimacy through their votes. In exchange, he gave people the "right" to choose the members of the parliament and a guarantee that their votes would bring about "national security, more honor to the nation and progress and development of the country" (16). Legitimization by the people is a necessity for the survival of the Islamic Republic of Iran.

Rejections

The analysis of IRIB regarding its use of international human rights language and the results obtained from the migrants are also noteworthy. The results suggest that most study participants are unable to recognize that human rights are broadcast on IRIB and that human rights language is ambiguously used when it concerns domestic human rights issues. Hence, there was a consensus that IRIB does not cover domestic human rights issues. Most, however, did recognize that some human rights issues related to foreign countries are covered on IRIB, even though they are also manipulated to meet political ends. Some 58% of the participants rated IRIB's coverage of human rights issues in other countries poor as opposed to 70% of the participants who rated IRIB's coverage of human rights in Iran poor. This recognition was limited to certain human rights principles and terms. It was evident that for most participants, "human rights" was a familiar term but what it exactly entails was ambiguous. The responses were, therefore, based on generally weak human rights knowledge.

Laura Fingerson suggests "[a]udiences use television and other media in everyday social interaction as vehicles for creating meaning and gaining understanding of the world around them" (17). The results suggest that the majority of the participants tended to dismiss what is shown on IRIB. However, in some instances, they unconsciously created the same meaning and understanding that was intended by the Islamic Republic of Iran to explain the execution of "miscreants," for example. That some participants voiced concern over the question of whether Israelis and Palestinians should have the same fundamental human rights and saw it as a political question rather than a human rights one illustrates that the Islamic Republic of Iran has been successful in intertwining politics and human rights just as it has enmeshed politics and religion.

Unfamiliarity with Human Rights Principles

The attitudes about Afghan refugees are somewhat striking as well because they seem to be an exception to the common trend of believing the opposite of what IRIB reports. The human rights situation of the Afghan refugees is suppressed on IRIB. IRIB is only tasked with encouraging repatriation of this "unwanted" group and warning the Iranians not to hire these refugees. The responses of participants against Afghan refugees in Iran could be based on cultural prejudices or the result of underlying prejudices reinforced by media and state policies.

Alternatively, the responses of the participants could be based on the personal experiences of the participants and have nothing to do with state policies and media. There are far too many examples of anti-immigration around the world, and Iran is no exception. According to Afsaneh Ashrafi and Haideh Moghissi "[R]eligious, linguistic, and cultural affinities between the migrants and the people of the host country" do not necessarily immune the migrants from "institutional discrimination and overt and covert prejudice" (18, 19).

During the interviews, one of the participants was distressed that foreign media only shows the dark side of Iran. He asked, "Why don't they show the good sides of Iran: for example, how the police in Iran maintain order and what benefits Iranians have in stadiums?" This participant's concern over such matters shows that the regime has either succeeded in keeping people uninformed about human rights in Iran or that most people do not care about the human rights of the whole society as long as they are not affected by it.

To illustrate this, let us focus on the two examples mentioned by the interviewee. Violence and disorder are on the rise in Iran. In addition, women are not allowed into the stadiums at all. The Supreme Leader of Iran, Ayatollah Khamenei, appoints the officials of the Islamic Republic of Iran Police (IRIP) and makes the final decisions for it. Due to Khamenei's lack of expertise in domestic policing, law enforcement has been negatively affected (20). According to Jalil Roshandel,

> The Police-110 rapid-response unit, established under the IRIP in 2000, is responsible for maintaining social order and responding to emergencies in urban areas. The unit frequently has raided social gatherings deemed threatening to domestic security or in violation of Islamic law (20).

The second example given by this interviewee was regarding the benefits provided to Iranians in stadiums. Even though there is no written rule, Iranian women are banned from attending stadiums. This participant was either ignorant that women are forbidden from entering stadiums or he firmly believed that women should be prohibited (21, 22).

Conclusion

The empirical findings in this research show that collection of statistics and exposure of human rights violations in Iran, although necessary for immediate protection of the Iranian citizens, are not sufficient to make a fundamental impact and bring about cultural change and widespread promotion of human rights principles. During the 2011 review of Iran's ICCPR periodic report, the Iranian delegation told the Committee that "[m]easures had been taken to create a culture of human rights awareness, including the dissemination of interviews and information in the media and the establishment of a human rights information centre that offered information in English and Persian." The delegation added,

> [t]he judiciary's department of public relations also provided relevant information. Human rights were a subject of education and research, and officials and academics had attended several conferences on the subject. A plan had been drawn up to increase public awareness of human rights and information had been provided to national human rights think tanks.[2]

According to this claim, the media, which includes television, should have developed a culture of human rights awareness. Unfortunately, there is no mechanism in place to monitor such claims.

Although the attitude of the Iranian delegation toward the UN has changed over the years from an antagonistic outlook to a more agonistic one, in 1993, it acknowledged the need for Iran to "improve its international image and to develop a genuine human rights dialogue."[3] The Islamic Republic has become somewhat open to having a human rights dialogue even though egregious human rights violations continue and worsen (7, 23, 24). This change in policy means that the Iranian regime has learned the human rights language and delivers precisely what the international community wishes to hear.

The research presented in this book is the first of its kind to look into text, images, and sound utilized by an authoritarian state's apparatus to determine how and whether the culture of human rights awareness, as claimed by the Iranian delegation to the UN, has been created. The results show that the human rights language has only been adopted with regard to the coverage of foreign news and even that is manipulated to meet Iran's political agenda. With such voluminous and time-sensitive human rights violations, most human rights NGOs are preoccupied with collecting statistics, with saving lives in imminent danger, and with bringing the Islamic Republic of Iran to account for its failure to protect the human rights of its citizens. Therefore, such claims regarding media, the dissemination of information to the Iranian people, and the state obligation to promote international human rights principles remain unchecked. The importance of the promotional aspect of the international human rights law, however, is abundantly clear from the empirical data produced in this book.

Future research can potentially focus more on the Iranian people and what they are being fed in terms of information. Future research could also focus on how and whether major host countries such as the United Kingdom, Canada, and the United States are assisting the newcomers to learn about international human rights laws and principles for them to become better informed about their rights and the rights of others. Educating migrants on universal values will assist them in integrating better into the global community and then transferring that knowledge to their connections in Iran. Based on the results, it is suggested that the UN, relevant organizations, and foreign offices of UN member states push a harder line against Iran not only on protection matters, but also on the promotion of human rights in its accepted and correct form. The application of pressure needs to be done continuously and systematically. Letting a state such as Iran cripple a nation on its most fundamental human rights to advance its political agenda is ominous and vexing in equal measure.

This research implies that the implementation of human rights within each state is different. It must be studied on a case-by-case basis and in a multidisciplinary fashion. The results of this research, however, could potentially contribute to the study of authoritarian states with hybrid political governance such as those formed after the 2011 Arab Spring.

Notes

1 The parliamentary elections were held to elect both the Islamic Consultative Assembly and the Assembly of Experts.
2 Paragraph 13, 2011 (CCPR/C/SR.2834).
3 Paragraph 34, 1993 (CERD/C/SR.990).

References

1. MehrNews. *Iran follows Imam Khomeini's path.* Mehr News Agency; January 31, 2016. Available from: http://en.mehrnews.com/news/114039/ Iran-follows-Imam-Khomeini-s-path.
2. HawzahNews. *Imam Khomeini and a united global Ummat.* 2010. Available from: http://www.hawzah.net/fa/Article/View/91447.
3. Khiabany G. Iranian media: The paradox of modernity. *Social Semiotics.* 2007;17(4):484 & 499.
4. Radio Farda. *IRIB: From Zarghami to Sarafraz.* 2014. Available from: http://www.radiofarda.com/content/f3-feature-on-iran-tv-managment/ 26680070.html.

5. SCRC. *Role of media and public opinion in organizing development and improvement of the Horizon of Development (With a perspective on radio and television).* 2007. Available from: http://mh.farhangoelm.ir/Articles/مهندسي-فرهنگي/1347.

6. Monshipouri M. Iran from 1979. In: Forsythe DP, editor. *Encyclopedia of human rights.* 5. Oxford: Oxford University Press; 2009:197.

7. Moinipour S. UN treaty-based bodies and the Islamic Republic of Iran: Human rights dialogue (1990–2016). *Cogent Social Sciences.* 2018;4(1):1–27.

8. Zahedi A. Concealing and revealing female hair: Veiling dynamics in contemporary Iran. In: Heath J, editor. *The veil: Women writers on its history, lore, and politics.* Berkeley & London: University of California Press; 2008:256–257.

9. The Lawrence Daily: Journal-World. Khomeini brands Israel 'Enemy of Humanity,' Rakes leftists, U.S. The Lawrence Daily: Journal-World, August 16, 1979. p. 23.

10. Department of Compilation Codification and Publication of Laws and Regulations. *Collection of laws and regulations: Islamic Republic of Iran Broadcasting.* Tehran: Publication and Printing Office; 2015. 1031 p. 200.

11. Boroumand L. *The meaning of coerced confessions in the Tehran show trials.* Human Rights & Democracy for Iran: A Project of the Abdorrahman Boroumand Foundation; 2009. Available from: https://www.iranrights.org/library/document/673/the-meaning-of-coerced-confessions-in-the-tehran-show-trials.

12. Bellin E. The robustness of authoritarianism in the Middle East: Exceptionalism in comparative perspective. *Comparative Politics.* 2004;36(2):143.

13. Pratt NC. *Democracy and authoritarianism in the Arab world.* Boulder, CO & London: Lynne Rienner Publishers; 2006. p. 14.

14. Oppenheim AN. *Questionnaire design, interviewing and attitude measurement.* London & New York: Continuum; 1992. p. 5.

15. Heinze E, Freedman R. Public awareness of human rights: Distortions in the mass media. *The International Journal of Human Rights.* 2010;14(4):492.

16. GooyaNews. *Khamenei: Opponents of the system must vote but have no right to candidacy.* 2016. Available from: http://news.gooya.com/politics/archives/2016/01/207463print.php.

17. Fingerson L. Active viewing—Girls' interpretations of family television programs. *Journal of Contemporary Ethnography.* 1999;28(4):391.

18. Ashrafi A, Moghissi H. Afghans in Iran: Asylum fatigue overshadows Islamic brotherhood. *Global Dialogue.* 2002;4(4):94.

19. Moinipour S. Refugees against refugees: The Iranian migrants' perception of the human rights of Afghans in Iran. *The International Journal of Human Rights.* 2017;21(7):823–37.

20. Roshandel J. National security. In: Curtis GE, Hooglund E, editors. *Iran: A country study.* Washington, DC: Federal Research Division, Library of Congress; 2008:278.

21. Shirazi F. Information and communication technology and women empowerment in Iran. *Telematics and Informatics.* 2011;29(2012):50.

22. Rouydad24. *The unwritten rule prohibiting the entry of women into the stadium must be lifted.* 2017. Available from: https://www.rouydad24.ir/fa/news/74624/قانون‌نان-نانشتم%C8%80%E2%-ممنوع‌تی-دورو-نانز-نان-به-وزرزش‌گاه-دیاب-دربش‌ادته-.دوش.

23. UN. *Ahmed Shaheed (Special Rapporteur) on Human Rights in Iran—Press Conference.* 2015. Available from: http://webtv.un.org/watch/ahmed-shaheed-special-rapporteur-on-human-rights-in-iran-press-conference/4582281878001.

24. Guardian. *UN says Iran more open to human rights dialogue despite alarming execution rates.* 2015. Available from: http://www.theguardian.com/world/2015/oct/26/iran-dialogue-human-rights-un-special-rapporteur.

Index

Note: Page numbers followed by "n" denote endnotes.